AAT

Synoptic Assessment
Level 4
Professional Accounting
Apprenticeship

EPA Exam Practice Kit
For Assessments from September 2024

Ninth edition 2024
ISBN 9781 0355 1775 6
eISBN 9781 0355 1776 3
Previous ISBN 9781 0355 0880 8

British Library Cataloguing-in-Publication Data
A catalogue record for this book is available
from the British Library

Published by

BPP Learning Media Ltd
BPP House, Aldine Place
142-144 Uxbridge Road
London W12 8AA

learningmedia.bpp.com

Printed in the United Kingdom

Your learning materials, published by BPP Learning Media Ltd, are printed on paper obtained from traceable sustainable sources.

BPP LEARNING MEDIA

Contents

Introduction

This is BPP Learning Media's AAT Exam Practice Kit for the *Professional Accounting Apprenticeship Level 4 Synoptic Assessment*. It is part of a suite of ground-breaking resources produced by BPP Learning Media for AAT assessments.

This Exam Practice Kit has been written in conjunction with the BPP Course Books and has been carefully designed to enable students to practise all of the relevant learning outcomes and assessment criteria that make up the *Professional Accounting Apprenticeship Level 4 Synoptic Assessment*. It is fully up to date as at March 2024 and reflects both the AAT's qualification specification and the practice assessment provided by the AAT as at April 2024.

This Exam Practice Kit contains these key features:

- Tasks corresponding to each assessment objective in the qualification specification and related task in the synoptic assessment. Some tasks in this Exam Practice Kit are designed for learning purposes, others are of assessment standard.
- AAT's EPAL4 practice assessment 1 and answers for the *Professional Accounting Apprenticeship Level 4 Synoptic Assessment* and further BPP practice assessments.

The emphasis in all tasks and assessments is on the practical application of the skills acquired.

VAT

You may find tasks throughout this Exam Practice Kit that need you to calculate or be aware of a rate of VAT. This is stated at 20% in these examples and questions.

Assessment method	Marking type	Duration of assessment
Computer based assessment	Partially computer/partially human marked	3 hours

Professional Accounting Apprenticeship Synoptic Assessment (PDSY)

Scope of content

Assessment objectives for the Level 4 synoptic assessment	Related learning objectives	Weighting
1 Demonstrate an understanding of the roles and responsibilities of the accounting function within an organisation and examine ways of preventing and detecting fraud and systemic weaknesses	**Systems and processes** LO1 Understand the role and responsibilities of the accounting function within an organisation LO2 Evaluate internal control systems	20%
2 Evaluate an organisation's accounting control systems and procedures	**Systems and processes** LO2 Evaluate internal control systems LO3 Evaluate an organisation's accounting system and underpinning procedures	20%

Assessment objectives for the Level 4 synoptic assessment		Related learning objectives	Weighting
3	Analyse an organisation's decision making and control using management accounting tools	**Systems and processes** LO1 Understand the role and responsibilities of the accounting function within an organisation LO2 Evaluate internal control systems LO3 Evaluate an organisation's accounting system and underpinning procedures LO4 Analyse recommendations made to improve an organisation's accounting system **Management accounting** LO1 Use appropriate financial and non-financial analysis to aid decision making LO2 Evaluate a range of cost management techniques to enhance value and aid decision making **Financial statements** LO2 Use ratio analysis to assess business performance	20%
4	Analyse an organisation's decision making and control using ratio analysis	**Systems and processes** LO1 Understand the role and responsibilities of the accounting function within an organisation LO2 Evaluate internal control systems LO4 Analyse recommendations made to improve an organisation's accounting system **Management accounting** LO1 Use appropriate financial and non-financial analysis to aid decision making **Financial statements** LO1 Understand the reporting frameworks and ethical principles that underpin financial reporting LO2 Use ratio analysis to assess business performance	20%

Assessment objectives for the Level 4 synoptic assessment	Related learning objectives	Weighting
5 Analyse the internal controls of an organisation and make recommendations	**Systems and processes** LO1 Understand the role and responsibilities of the accounting function within an organisation LO2 Evaluate internal control systems LO3 Evaluate an organisation's accounting system and underpinning procedures LO4 Analyse recommendations made to improve an organisation's accounting system **Management accounting** LO1 Use appropriate financial and non-financial analysis to aid decision making LO2 Evaluate a range of cost management techniques to enhance value and aid decision making **Financial statements** LO1 Understand the reporting frameworks and ethical principles that underpin financial reporting	20%
Total		**100%**

Approaching the assessment

When you sit the assessment it is very important that you follow the on-screen instructions. This means you need to carefully read the instructions, both on the introduction screens and during specific tasks.

When you access the assessment you should be presented with an introductory screen with information similar to that shown below (taken from the introductory screen from one of the AAT's EPAL4 practice assessments for the *Professional Accounting Apprenticeship Level 4 Synoptic Assessment).*

You have **3 hours** to complete this **Professional Diploma Synoptic** practice assessment.

- This assessment contains **5 tasks** and you should attempt to complete **every** task.
- Each task is independent. You will not need to refer to your answers to previous tasks.
- The total number of marks for this assessment is **100**.
- Read every task carefully to make sure you understand what is required.
- Where the date is relevant, it is given in the task data.
- Both minus signs and brackets can be used to indicate negative numbers **unless** task instructions slate otherwise.
- You must use a full stop to indicate a decimal point. For example, write 100.57 **not** 100,57 or 10057.
- You may use a comma to indicate a number in the thousands, but you don't have to. For example, 10000 and 10,000 are both acceptable.
- You will need to double click to enter values into a gapfill or cell within a table.

The actual instructions will vary depending on the assessment you are sitting. It is very important you read the instructions on the introductory screen and apply them in the assessment. You don't want to lose marks when you know the correct answer just because you have not entered it in the right format.

In general, the rules set out in the AAT practice assessments for this subject will apply in the real assessment, but you should carefully read the information on this screen again in the real assessment, just to make sure. This screen may also confirm the VAT rate used, if applicable.

A full stop is needed to indicate a decimal point. We would recommend using minus signs to indicate negative numbers (unless instructed otherwise by the task) and leaving out the comma signs to indicate thousands. This results in a lower number of key strokes and less margin for error when working under time pressure. Having said that, you can use whatever is easiest for you as long as you operate within the rules set out for the assessment.

You have to show competence throughout the assessment and you should therefore complete all of the tasks. Don't leave questions unanswered.

In some assessments, written or complex tasks may be human marked. In this case you are given a blank space or table to enter your answer into. You are told in the assessments which tasks these are. **Note.** There may be none if all answers are marked by the computer. If these involve calculations, it is a good idea to decide in advance how you are going to lay out your answers to such tasks by practising answering them on a Word document, and certainly you should try all such tasks in this EPA Exam Practice Kit and in the AAT's environment using the practice assessment.

When asked to fill in tables, or gaps, never leave any blank even if you are unsure of the answer. Fill in your best estimate.

Note that for some assessments where there is a lot of scenario information or tables of data provided (eg budget information) you may need to access these via 'pop-ups'. Instructions will be provided on how you can bring up the necessary data during the assessment.

Take note of any task specific instructions once you are in the assessment. For example you may be asked to enter a date in a certain format or to enter a number to a certain number of decimal places.

Pay close attention to the language used in the question. Key words such as 'evaluate', 'justify', 'compare' and 'explain' will be key to answering the question in the most appropriate manner. The AAT website has a useful 'Writing Skills' presentation and quiz (www.aat.org.uk/learning-portal) which will introduce you to the various terms used, and help to give you guidance on your writing technique.

AAT makes pre-release material about the scenario in this synoptic assessment available for you to read before you sit it. This will be available on the AAT website (student login required) at www.aat.org.uk/learning-portal (refer to Professional Accounting Professional Diploma Synoptic Assessment (EPAL4).

During the assessment you can access this pre-release material, plus other relevant information provided within the assessment, via 'pop-up windows'. Instructions will be provided on how you can bring up the necessary information during the assessment. For instance in one of the AAT practice assessments the following instructions are given:

Scenario and pre-release material

The real live scenario will be available on the AAT website. Please note, it will **not** be the same as the scenario in the practice assessment.

Pop-ups

The pre-release material is made available in every task via pop-up windows which can be opened by clicking on the links on the menu provided.

Other relevant reference material is shown in pop-up windows throughout the assessment. You can open these pop-up windows at any point by clicking on buttons that look like this:

You can open, close and re-open the pop-ups as often as you want and you can position them anywhere on the screen.

Finally, take note of any task specific instructions once you are in the assessment. For example you may be asked to enter a date in a certain format or to enter a number to a certain number of decimal places.

Grading

As part of their End Point Assessment (EPA), apprentices will be expected to complete:

- a synoptic assessment; and
- a portfolio and reflective discussion or written statement, which exhibits a range of evidence produced in the workplace to demonstrate they have met the knowledge, skills and behaviours (KSBs) specified in the standard.

Weighting of individual assessment components

As shown in the table below, there will be two successful grades for the apprenticeship - pass and distinction. The grade is determined by the result of the synoptic assessment.

Assessment component	Component grade
Assessment method 1: Synoptic assessment	Fail, pass or distinction
Assessment method 2: Portfolio and reflective discussion or written statement	Fail or pass To pass, evidence must be produced to show that all the goals have been demonstrated and relate to the submitted portfolio of evidence

The synoptic assessment will be partially computer marked and partially human-marked by AAT markers. Results will be available six weeks from the date of assessment, following quality assurance processes by AAT.

Re-sits

The AAT Professional Accounting Apprenticeship synoptic assessment is not subject to re-sit restrictions.

You should only be entered for an assessment when you are well-prepared and you expect to pass the assessment.

AAT qualifications

The material in this book may support the following AAT qualifications:

AAT Professional Accounting Apprenticeship Level 4

Supplements

From time to time we may need to publish supplementary materials to one of our titles. This can be for a variety of reasons, from a small change in the AAT unit guidance to new legislation coming into effect between editions.

You should check our supplements page regularly for anything that may affect your learning materials. All supplements are available free of charge on our supplements page on our website at:

https://learningmedia.bpp.com/pages/resources-for-students

Improving material and removing errors

BPP Learning Media do everything possible to ensure the material is accurate and up to date when sending to print. In the event that any errors are found after the print date, they are uploaded to the following website:

https://learningmedia.bpp.com/pages/errata

Question Bank

Chapter 1 – The accounting function

Task 1.1

Johnson Services Ltd (JSL) is a large company which provides marketing services to small businesses. Each branch performs all its own accounting on a stand-alone laptop and emails results to the two directors once a month. The company has grown quickly and the directors are now concerned that its accounting function and systems are failing to support the business fully. They have approached you for some guidance.

(a) **Complete the following statement that you make to the directors.**

If you want your accounting system to be integrated then you need to

(1) | Centralise it ▼ | . A key benefit of integrating the company's accounting system is that you can ensure every area of the business complies with relevant

(2) | Laws & Regulations ▼ | .

Picklist (1):

centralise it

~~decentralise it~~ ✓

Picklist (2):

laws and regulations
operational objectives

(b) **For each of the following criteria, identify whether a centralised or a decentralised accounting function is better for JSL.**

Criterion	Centralised accounting function ✓	Decentralised accounting function ✓
More economies of scope	✓	✗
Better communication with business units	✗	✓ ✗
Better placed to produce group accounts	✓	
More economies of scale	✓	

Task 1.2

For each of the following tasks, identify which person will be responsible for their completion.

Task	Responsible party
Preparation of budgetary control reports	Management Account ▼
Maintain accounting ledgers	Financial ▼
Cash management	Treasury Manager ▼

Picklist:

Financial accountant
Management accountant
~~Treasury manager~~

Task 1.3

For each of the following parties, identify their responsibility within a limited company.

Party	Responsibility
External auditors	report whether FS show a true $ fair view ▼
Accounting function	Maintain Acc Sy ▼
Directors	Prepare FS for Comp ▼

Picklist:

Maintain the accounting system
Prepare financial statements for the company
Report whether the financial statements show a true and fair view

Task 1.4

The directors of JSL have decided to have a centralised accounting system with the accounting function operating from its headquarters building. They have identified a number of possible candidates for the role of chief accountant but each candidate has different levels of experience and qualifications. JSL's directors have approached you seeking guidance on the ethical and professional qualities for which they should be looking in their chief accountant.

(a) If JSL's chief accountant acts diligently they are complying with part of which professional principle?

	✓
Professional behaviour	
Objectivity	
Professional competence and due care	✓
Integrity	

One of JSL's directors takes you aside to tell you about a problem encountered by one of the accounting function's staff Kim, an AAT member. A supplier of JSL contacted Kim and asked her to give the supplier a list of JSL's customers so that it could send the customers a mailshot. In return the supplier offered Kim a trip to Disney World. The director only discovered this when Kim told him.

(b) Answer the following questions.

Which of the fundamental principles is threatened for Kim by this offer?

Confidentiality ▼

Picklist:

Confidentiality
Integrity
Professional competence and due care

What action should Kim take?

refuse $ Decline ▼

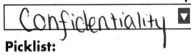

Picklist:

She can accept but must advise all the directors
She can accept but must have no further dealings with the supplier
She may reveal the information but must decline the trip
She must refuse to reveal the information and decline the trip –
She must resign from JSL

Task 1.5

After identifying a variety of control activities for its accounting system, the chief accountant of JSL has raised a query about what type of security control each control activity represents. They are keen to ensure in particular that the passwords used within the accounting function are as strong as possible, but require further guidance on this.

(a) For each of the following control activities used by JSL, identify what type of control it is.

Control activity	Type of control
Securing invoices in a locked cupboard	Physical ▼
Authorising changes to standing data	Integrity ▼

Picklist:

Physical control
Integrity control

(b) Which of the following is the most secure password for use by JSL's accounting function?

	✓
Mmmeee	
82s09PQ#	✓
1357abcd	

Task 1.6

Within JSL's accounting function, the duties of sales invoicing, sales ledger and credit control are separated from each other. The person responsible for credit control, Iqbal Hussein, discovers that two sales invoices have been raised in respect of the same sale. Both invoices have been recorded in the sales day book and posted to the general and sales ledgers.

What is the correct action for Iqbal to take?

	✓
Reverse the duplicate entries and advise the sales ledger team of his action	
Inform the sales invoicing team of the error	✓
Report the error to the chief accountant	
Prepare a credit note and send it to the customer	

Task 1.7

Iqbal has asked you to tell him whether the following errors would be detected by reconciling the sales ledger to the sales ledger control account.

Error	Detected by reconciliation?
A batch of purchase invoices posted to the sales ledger control account	Yes
A pricing error in a sales invoice	NO
VAT on a sales invoice posted to insurance rather than the VAT control account	NO
A sales invoice posted to the wrong customer account	NO
A sales invoice credited to the customer's account	Yes

Picklist:

Yes
No

Task 1.8

The chief accountant of JSL has informed you that the company is intending to reduce costs by streamlining the accounting function and reducing the number of staff. They are considering getting Iqbal to take over the sales invoicing and sales ledger functions, in addition to his responsibility for credit control.

Critically comment on this suggestion.

Task 1.9

Star Supplies Ltd is a rapidly expanding family-run business based in South Lincolnshire, who supply local fresh fruit and vegetable boxes to over 150 retail customers in Cambridgeshire and Lincolnshire. The managing director, Elysia Parker, is considering the strategy of the business over the next five years. She has come to you for some advice.

> 'I have heard about companies having a mission statement. Please can you explain what this means? We are also looking at developing our business and have considered two alternative directions:

- Growing our own produce; we currently rely on a number of local farmers, but cannot always get what we need, so we are considering growing our own range of King Edward potatoes and heritage carrots.
- Using our delivery network to supply homemade pizzas to the local area.'

Explain what a mission statement is, focusing on the three main elements it should have to be effective. Explain how a mission statement could be useful for future strategic planning, such as considering the expansion options for the business.

Task 1.10

Iqbal has noted that Tripot Ltd (TL), a customer of JSL, is slow in paying its outstanding debt to JSL. From conversations with staff at TL he suspects that TL is experiencing serious financial difficulties. Iqbal's friend, Josh Jones, is considering selling goods on credit to TL. Iqbal has told Josh that he suspects TL is experiencing financial difficulties and will be unable to pay him.

Identify and explain which of the ethical principles Iqbal has breached by this action.

Task 1.11

Which THREE of the following statements are MOST likely to be found in a sustainability report of JSL?

	✓
A discussion of sales figures for the main three products of JSL	
Highlighting the employee volunteering opportunities from a team helping to re-turf a school football pitch	✓
Reporting on the recycling efforts within the office environment	✓
Reporting any incidents of money laundering and how the organisation seeks to change its controls going forward	✓

Task 1.12

Which ONE of the following statements about the trial balance is correct?

	✓
It is a memorandum account to keep track of amounts owing from individual customers and owed to individual suppliers.	
It will detect all bookkeeping errors.	
It is prepared after closing off the general ledger accounts and before preparing the final accounts.	✓
It will always include a suspense account.	

X

Task 1.13

This task is about accounting adjustments.

You are a trainee accounting technician reporting to a managing partner in an accounting practice. You are working on the accounting records of a business client.

An initial trial balance has been drawn up and balanced using a suspense account. You now need to make some corrections and adjustments for the year ended 31 December 20X7.

You may ignore VAT in this task.

Depreciation on the plant must be calculated. Plant is depreciated at 20% per year on a straight-line basis assuming no residual value.

(a) Calculate the depreciation charge on plant for the year.

£	6480

32400 × 20%

6980

(b) (i) Record this adjustment into the extract from the adjusted trial balance below.

(ii) Make the following further adjustments.

You will NOT need to enter adjustments on every line. Do NOT enter zeros into unused cells.

- The carriage outwards balance of £460 was omitted from the trial balance. The corresponding entry (a cheque payment) is correctly included in the cash book.
- The purchases balance was incorrectly transferred to the trial balance. The balance should be £88,540 and not £89,430.
- The payment of office expenses of £70 has been reversed in both general ledger accounts.

Extract from the adjusted trial balance

Ledger account	Initial trial balance		Adjustments	
	Debit £	Credit £	Debit £	Credit £
Bank	5,321			140
Carriage outwards			460	
Depreciation charges			6480	
Irrecoverable debts	632			
Office expenses	52,832		140	
Payables ledger control account		11,230		
Plant at cost	32,400			
Plant accumulated depreciation		6,480		6480
Prepaid expenses	305			
Purchases	89,430			890
Receivables ledger control account	16,230			
Rent	12,520			
Sales		104,502		
Suspense		430	890	460
VAT		9,320		

Task 2.1

Complete the following statement:

Allocating a payment from one customer to another customer's account in order to balance the books and detract from a shortfall is called [teeming & Lading ▼].

Picklist:

identity fraud
inflation
reconciliation and review
teeming and lading

Task 2.2

Which of the following are the THREE types of fraud specified in the Fraud Act 2006?

	✓
False representation	✓
Failure to segregate duties	
Failure to disclose information	✓
Abuse of position	✓
Duress and undue influence	

Task 2.3

Identify what, if any, effect each of the following systemic weaknesses in an accounting system will have on reported profit.

Systemic weakness	Understatement of reported profit ✓	Overstatement of reported profit ✓
Overvaluation of inventory at the period end		
Creating an unnecessary allowance for doubtful debts		
Fictitious sales		
Not writing off irrecoverable debts		
Overstating expenses		

Task 2.4

Identify whether each of the following systemic weaknesses in an accounting system could lead to misappropriation of assets and/or misstatement in the financial statements.

Systemic weakness	Misappropriation of assets ✓	Misstatement in the financial statements ✓
Leaving offices where computers are held unlocked	✓	
Failing to maintain an asset register		✓
Omitting inventory from the annual physical count		✓
Creating a fictitious employee on the payroll	✓	✓
Failing to chase unpaid debts		✓

Task 2.5

Complete the following statement:

Segregation of duties is a type of [▼] over fraud in the accounting system.

Staff control

Picklist:

application control
management control
physical control
staff control

Task 2.6

You have been asked to review the adequacy of the control in Hansom Ltd's sales procedures. Your review has established the following information.

The company operates an integrated accounting system which includes a sales accounting module. The sales manager is responsible for managing sales activities.

Ordering and despatch:

- All sales, except those for cash, must be documented on an official customer order. The order should state the agreed price, if known.
- Customer orders must be reviewed and signed by the sales manager.
- Large orders must be signed by the finance director.
- Five copies of the order form are printed. Once signed, the original is sent to the customer as an acknowledgement. A copy printed on yellow paper is sent to the accounts receivable clerk. A pink copy is sent to production and a green copy is sent to despatch. The orange copy is retained by the individual who took the order.
- When the goods are completed, production signs the pink copy and sends it to despatch.
- When the goods are sent out, despatch signs the green copy and sends it, with the pink copy, to the accounts receivable clerk.

New customers:

- New customers are contacted by the sales manager. She asks for a trade reference and banking details, and offers credit terms.
- She usually offers credit terms as either of the following:
  - One month from the end of the month in which delivery takes place
  - A 5% discount for payment within 21 days of delivery

  However, terms are subject to negotiation.

Accounting:

- All sales invoices are raised by the accounts receivable clerk. He matches yellow, pink and green copy orders and prepares the invoices for sending to the customer.
- He posts the invoices to the computerised accounting system.
- He answers queries from customers, issuing credit notes when appropriate.
- Most customers pay through the bankers automated clearing system (BACS). The accounts receivable clerk checks the bank account weekly and posts receipts to the ledger accounts.

Identify as many systemic weaknesses in the company's internal controls for handling sales on credit as you can, and explain how each weakness that you have identified could create a problem for the company.

Note. You are **not** required to make recommendations to change procedures.

No.	Weakness	Potential problem
1		
2		
3		
4		
5		
6		
7		
8		
9		
10		

Task 2.7

You have been asked to review the adequacy of the control in Hansom Ltd's payroll procedures. Your review has established the following information.

The company operates an integrated accounting system which includes a payroll accounting module. The accounts manager, based at the head office, is responsible for managing payroll activities. The payroll clerk, based at the factory, performs day-to-day payroll tasks.

The payroll clerk:

- Maintains standing data on employees
- Records each employee's hours at work where this information is relevant and available
- Calculates gross pay and deductions
- Prepares the wages control account
- Prepares the BACS payments each month to employees and HMRC
- Reconciles total pay and deductions in the wages control account

Once a month the accounts manager reviews total payroll cost against budget and investigates unexpected variances.

Which THREE of the following types of control activity are weakest in Hansom Ltd's payroll system?

	✓
Physical controls	
Segregation of duties	✓
Management controls	
Supervisory controls	✓
Organisation	
Authorisation (approval) of transactions	✓
Arithmetic and bookkeeping checks	
Personnel controls	

Task 2.8

Insyst Furniture Ltd (IFL) has grown rapidly in the last two years since its formation and now has a forecast revenue of £10m. The CEO has asked for your advice on the purchases system, which she feels may not be adequate for this size of company.

You have been told the following:

(1) When materials are required for production, the production manager sends a handwritten note to the buying manager. The buying manager finds a suitable supplier and raises a purchase order. The purchase order is signed by the CEO;

(2) Materials for production are received by the goods received department, who issue a sequentially numbered goods received note (GRN) and send a copy to the purchases ledger clerk. There is no system for recording receipt of other goods and services;

(3) The purchases ledger clerk receives the purchase invoice, matches it with the goods received note and purchase order (if available). The CEO authorises the invoice for posting to the purchases ledger;

(4) The purchases ledger clerk analyses the invoice and posts it to the purchase ledger;

(5) The purchases ledger clerk prepares the cheques and remittances, and posts the cheques to the purchases ledger and cash book; and

(6) The CEO signs the cheques, and the purchases ledger clerk sends the cheques and remittances to the suppliers.

Identify SIX weaknesses in controls in IFL's purchases system and the implications of those weaknesses.

No.	Weakness	Potential problem
1		
2		
3		
4		
5		
6		

Task 2.9

The CEO of TML has approached you for advice on its payroll system. The company has grown rapidly and now has over 200 employees. There are concerns that the payroll system may not be adequate.

You have obtained the following information:

(1) On Monday mornings each employee takes a blank time card from a pile and writes his or her name and number at the top. Each day of the week they record their starting and finishing times. The following Monday each department supervisor collects the cards and forwards them to the wages clerk.

(2) Personnel and wages records are maintained by the wages clerk. From the time cards he calculates the hours worked by each employee and enters them into a payroll program on the computer. This program, using data from personnel records as to wage rates and deductions, produces the weekly payroll and a payslip for each employee.

(3) The wages clerk prepares a cheque requisition for the total net pay for the week, which is sent to the company accountant together with a copy of the payroll. The accountant draws up the cheque, made payable to cash, and has it countersigned by a director. The wages clerk takes the cheque to the bank and uses the cash to prepare the wage packets. Wage packets are given to the department supervisors for distribution to the employees in their department as they see fit.

(4) There is no personnel department. Each department supervisor has the authority to engage new employees and to determine changes in wage rates with the verbal consent of a director.

Identify SIX weaknesses in controls in TML's wages system and the implications of those weaknesses.

No.	Weakness	Potential problem
1		
2		
3		
4		
5		
6		

Chapter 3 – Decision making and control

Task 3.1

Complete the following statement.

The [FO ▼] total variance may be analysed into expenditure, efficiency and capacity variances.

Picklist:

fixed overheads
labour
materials
variable overheads

Task 3.2

Yombo Ltd makes the product X07. The standard and actual results for the month of June 20X1 are as follows.

		Standard		Actual
Production (units of X07)		14,000		13,500
Direct materials	17,500 litres	£28,875	16,800 litres	£106,000
Direct labour	3,500 hours	£59,500	3,650 hours	£65,700
Fixed overheads (absorbed on a unit basis)		£77,000		£79,500
Total		£165,375		£251,200

Complete the following statements:

(a) The standard quantity of labour per unit is [ ] minutes.

(b) The standard quantity of materials needed to produce 13,500 units of X07 is [ ] litres.

(c) The standard labour hours to produce 12,000 units of X07 is [ ] hours.

(d) The standard labour cost to produce 13,500 units of X07 is

£ [ ].

(e) The standard overhead absorption rate per unit is

£ [ ].

Task 3.3

Statham Ltd purchases 3,700 kilograms of material at a cost of £10,915. The total material price variance is £1,665 adverse.

(a) Complete the following statement.

The standard cost per kilogram is | £ | |.

Statham Ltd purchases and uses 200,000 litres of a different material at a cost of £0.55 per litre. The budgeted production was 22,000 units which requires 220,000 litres of material at a total standard cost of £132,000. The actual production was 19,000 units.

(b) Complete the following statement.

The material usage variance is | £ | | ▼ |.

Picklist:

adverse
favourable

Statham Ltd expects to produce 10,000 units of X using 6,000 hours of labour. The standard cost of labour is £15 per hour. The actual output was 12,000 units. 6,900 hours of labour were worked and 7,300 hours were paid at a total cost of £105,850.

(c) Complete the following statements.

The total labour efficiency variance is | £ | | ▼ |.

Picklist:

adverse
favourable

The idle time variance is | £ | | ▼ |.

Picklist:

adverse
favourable

Task 3.4

Bert Ltd manufactures product RPB. Bert Ltd operates a standard cost system in which production overheads are fixed and absorbed on a unit basis.

The budgeted activity is for the production of 28,000 units at a total fixed production cost of £350,000. The actual volume of production was 30,000 units and the fixed overhead expenditure variance was £35,000 favourable.

Complete the following statements.

The fixed overhead volume variance is | £ | | ▼ |.

Picklist:

adverse
favourable

The actual fixed production overheads incurred were | £ | |.

Task 3.5

Randall Ltd manufactures product RTF. The budgeted activity and actual results for the month are as follows.

	Budget	Actual
Production units (RTF)	64,000	67,000
Direct labour costs	£5,760,000	£5,896,000
Fixed overheads	£3,840,000	£3,950,000

Overheads are absorbed on a labour hour basis and the budget uses 480,000 labour hours. The actual labour hours used to produce 67,000 units totalled 536,000 labour hours.

Calculate the following variances.

Variance	Amount £	Adverse/Favourable
Fixed overhead capacity		▼
Fixed overhead efficiency		▼

Picklist:

adverse
favourable

Task 3.6

The following budgetary control report has been provided for Pelling Ltd together with the variances calculated below.

	Budget		Actual	
Production (units)		12,400		13,600
Direct materials	37,200 kg	£130,200	37,400 kg	£112,200
Direct labour	24,800 hours	£223,200	28,560 hours	£285,600
Fixed overheads		£234,000		£221,000
Total cost		£587,400		£618,800

Variance	Amount
Direct materials price	18,700 F
Direct materials usage	11,900 F
Direct labour rate	28,560 A
Direct labour efficiency	Not yet calculated
Fixed overhead expenditure	Not yet calculated

Pelling Ltd normally prepares an operating statement under standard absorption costing principles but the financial director has asked you to prepare one under standard marginal costing principles.

Place each variance into the correct column (favourable or adverse) and complete the table.

			£
Budgeted variable cost for actual production			
Budgeted fixed cost			
Total budgeted cost for actual production			
Variance	**Favourable £**	**Adverse £**	
Direct materials price			
Direct materials usage			
Direct labour rate			
Direct labour efficiency			
Fixed overhead expenditure			
Fixed overhead volume	▼	▼	
Total variance			
Actual cost of actual production			

Picklist:

22,645
N/A

Task 3.7

Keta Ltd operates a standard costing system and uses raw material C2X, which is a global commodity. The standard price was set based upon a market price of £450 per litre when the material price index for C2X was 120.50. The following information has been gathered:

- The price index increased to 126.525 in June 20X3.
- The raw material price variance for June was £375,000 adverse.
- 12,500 litres of material C2X were purchased in June.

Complete the statements below. In order to calculate your answers, you should split the raw material price variance into two components by calculating the part of the variance explained by the change in the price index and the part of the variance not explained by the change in the price index.

(a) The part of the variance explained by the increase in the price index is | £ | | .

(b) The part of the variance not explained by the increase in the price index is | £ | | .

(c) The percentage increase in the index is | | %.

Keta Ltd also uses product Z4QX and has collected data from the last few months in order to forecast the cost per kilogram of Z4QX in the next period.

	April 20X3	May 20X3	June 20X3
Cost per kilogram of Z4QX (£)	1,457.92	1,593.66	1,729.40

(d) Complete the table below to forecast the expected price of product Z4QX in September and December 20X3.

	September 20X3	December 20X3
Cost per kilogram of Z4QX (£)		

A colleague has calculated the least squares regression line (the line of best fit) for a different product as **y = 24.69 + 2.14x**, where y is the cost per kilogram (in £) and x is the monthly period. June 20X3 is period 41.

(e) Complete the statement below.

The forecast cost per kilogram, using the regression line, for September 20X3 is | £ | | .

Task 3.8

You have been provided with the following information for Vocco Ltd, which manufactures a product called Becks, for the month just ended.

	Budget		Actual	
Production (units)		20,000		21,000
Direct materials	80,000 kg	£880,000	83,000 kg	£954,500

The finance director has asked you to write a note to help in the training of a junior accounting technician. The notes are to explain the calculation of the total direct material variance and how this variance can be split into a price variance and a usage variance.

Prepare a note explaining the total direct material variance and how it can be split into a price variance and usage variance. Calculations should be used to illustrate the explanation.

Task 3.9

You have been provided with the following information for two scenarios involving a company which operates an absorption costing system.

	Scenario 1	Scenario 2
Sales volume (units)	120,000	150,000
	£	£
Revenue	1,680,000	1,800,000
Gross profit	600,000	450,000
Profit from operations	275,000	200,000
Capital employed	2,298,400	2,100,340
Inventory	147,950	167,500

(a) Calculate the following performance indicators for Scenario 1 and 2.

	Scenario 1	Scenario 2
Return on capital employed		
Inventory holding period in days		
Sales price per unit		
Full production cost per unit		

(b) Complete the table below for Scenario 3.

	Scenario 3
Capital employed (£)	175,000
Return on capital employed (%)	13
Profit margin (%)	14
Gearing (%)	32.75
Profit (to the nearest £)	
Sales revenue (to the nearest £)	

(c) Fill in the boxes with the appropriate options to show how to calculate the gearing. If there is more than one correct answer, either answer will achieve full marks.

[ ]		
———	×	[ ]
[ ]		

Options:

Total non-current liabilities	Profit	365
Capital employed	Total equity	100
Total non-current liabilities plus Total equity	Total non-current liabilities less Total equity	Revenue

Task 3.10

Alpha Ltd makes two products, Tig and Tag. The following information is available for the next month.

	Product Tig £ per unit	Product Tag £ per unit
Selling price	4,000	4,950
Variable costs		
Material cost (£400 per kilogram)	2,400	3,000
Labour cost	400	600
Total variable cost	2,800	3,600
Fixed costs		
Production cost	450	450
Administration cost	300	300
Total fixed costs	750	750
Profit per unit	450	600
Monthly demand	200 units	300 units

The materials are in short supply in the coming month and only 3,000 kilograms of material will be available from the existing supplier.

(a) Complete the table below.

	Product Tig £	Product Tag £
The contribution per unit is		
The contribution per kilogram of materials is		

(b) Complete the following statement.

The optimal production order for products Tig and Tag is [▼].

Picklist:

Tag then Tig
Tig then Tag

(c) Complete the table below for the optimal production mix.

	Product Tig	Product Tag
Production in units		

(d) Complete the table below for the total contribution for each product.

	Product Tig £	Product Tag £
Total contribution		

Alpha Ltd has been approached by another materials supplier who can supply up to 500 kilograms of material at a cost per kilogram of £500. This is a premium of £100 above the normal cost per kilogram.

(e) Complete the table below.

Should Alpha Ltd purchase the additional material?	Give a reason
(1) ▼	(2) ▼

Picklist (1):

Yes
No

Picklist (2):

The additional cost per kilogram is greater than the contribution per kilogram

The additional cost per kilogram is greater than the contribution per unit

The additional cost per kilogram is less than the contribution per kilogram

The additional cost per kilogram is less than the contribution per unit

Task 3.11

Alpha Ltd is considering designing a new product, product BPT, and will use target costing to arrive at the target cost of the product. You have been given the following information.

- The price at which the product will be sold has not yet been decided.
- It has been estimated that if the price is set at £40 the demand will be 500,000 units, and if the price is set at £50 the demand will be 430,000 units.
- The costs of production include fixed production costs of £8,500,000 which will give a production capacity of 500,000 units.
- In order to produce above this level the fixed costs will step up by £1,500,000.
- The required profit margin is 30%.
- The variable cost per unit is £13 for the production volume of 430,000 units.
- For production volume of 500,000 units the variable cost will be £12 per unit.

(a) Complete the table for both levels of demand.

	Sales price £40	Sales price £50
The target total production cost per unit		
The target fixed production cost per unit		
The target total fixed production cost		

(b) Complete the following statement.

Alpha should set the price at [▼] in order to achieve the target profit margin.

Picklist:

£40
£50

Task 3.12

You have been provided with the following information for Beta Ltd.

Current position

The price is currently £22 per unit. At this price demand is 150,000 units each year. The advertising costs are currently £500,000 per year. The current factory can produce a maximum of 400,000 units per annum. The labour and material costs are the only variable costs.

Proposed position

The price will reduce to £18 per unit. Advertising costs will increase to £750,000 per year and it is expected that this will increase demand to 300,000 units per year. The factory will still be limited to 400,000 units per year. The labour and material costs are the only variable costs.

The forecast information for each scenario is shown below.

Statement of profit or loss	Current position (actual)	Proposed position (forecast)
Sales price per unit	£22	£18
Sales volume	150,000	300,000
	£	£
Revenue	3,300,000	5,400,000
Direct materials	750,000	1,200,000
Direct labour	900,000	1,800,000
Fixed production costs	600,000	600,000
Total cost of sales	2,250,000	3,600,000
Gross profit	1,050,000	1,800,000
Fixed advertising costs	500,000	750,000
Administration costs	300,000	400,000
Profit	250,000	650,000
Material cost per unit	£5.00	£4.00
Labour cost per unit	£6.00	£6.00
Fixed production cost per unit	£4.00	£2.00
Fixed advertising cost per unit	£3.33	£2.50
Gross profit margin	31.82%	33.33%
Profit margin	7.58%	12.04%
Inventory of finished goods	£350,000	
Trade receivables	£500,000	

Draft a report for the finance director covering the following:

(a) An explanation of why the gross profit margin for the proposed position is higher than the current position, referring to the following:

- **Sales volume**
- **Materials cost**
- **Labour cost**
- **Fixed production costs**

(b) An explanation of what is likely to happen to the current asset position of the business by considering the following:

- **Inventory levels (include a prediction of inventory level based upon the current inventory holding period)**
- **Trade receivable levels (include a prediction of the level based upon current trade receivables collection period)**

To:	Finance director	**Subject:**	Variances
From:	Accounting technician	**Date:**	Today

(a) Sales volume

Materials cost

Labour cost

Fixed production costs

(b) Inventory levels

Trade receivables levels

Task 3.13

Seismic Security Systems Ltd (SSSL) is a rapidly expanding company which sells security cameras to small and medium-sized businesses. The CEO, Teresa Maynot, has asked you to review the sales system, which she currently oversees, and suggest how it should be updated in light of the company's growth. She has provided you with the following information about the existing system:

Sales are made through a team of five sales staff. As they are thought to know the customers best, they are responsible for assessing the creditworthiness of new customers and setting their initial credit limit. Sales staff are also able to make decisions on the amount of sales discount to grant to customers, up to a maximum of 20%, which they then record in the customer's master file.

Sales staff then email the despatch and accounting departments to initiate the despatch and invoicing of the goods. The company's terms of sale are 30 days, and at the end of each month a list of outstanding receivables over 120 days are passed to the sales staff for them to follow up with the relevant customers.

(a) Suggest TWO new roles which SSSL should recruit in order to improve the sales system. Identify for each role the tasks they should take over and why.

(b) Explain TWO potential problems which SSSL might face after recruiting individuals to these roles.

Task 3.14

Gritby Fish Co manufactures three products – Prawn, Roe and Bass. The net profit from these is shown below:

	Prawn £	Roe £	Bass £	Total £
Sales	100,000	80,000	120,000	300,000
Variable costs	60,000	50,000	70,000	180,000
Contribution	40,000	30,000	50,000	120,000
Fixed costs	34,000	36,000	40,000	110,000
Profit/loss	6,000	(6,000)	10,000	10,000

Gritby is concerned about the performance of Roe and is deciding whether it should cease production of them in order to produce a new product, Codlings.

The forecasted profit generated by Codlings is shown below:

	Codlings £
Sales	90,000
Variable costs	66,000
Contribution	24,000
Fixed costs	16,000
Profit/loss	8,000

Additional information

- The fixed costs associated with the production of Roe are £10,000.
- Directly attributable fixed costs of Codlings are £12,000.

Critically appraise, using numerical evidence where appropriate, whether Gritby Fish Co should cease the production of Roe and start selling Codlings.

Task 3.15

Daisy Ltd owns two subsidiaries, Dandelion and Blossom.

Dandelion manufactures bespoke furniture, relying on local suppliers of sustainable wood and Blossom makes a mid-range equivalent, sourcing the raw materials from overseas. Both are sold to local, independent retailers, although customers do not buy from both companies, due to the different target audiences.

The forecasts for both factories for the year ending 31 December 20X5 are below:

	Dandelion £000		Blossom £000	
Revenue	2,200		2,850	
Direct materials	660		784	
Direct labour	440		448	
Fixed production overheads	220		420	
Cost of sales	1,320		1,652	
Gross profit	880	40%	1,198	42%
Sales and distribution costs	520		640	
Administration costs	210		250	
Profit from operations	150	6.8%	308	10.8%

Other information:

- Inventories are of raw materials and will remain unchanged throughout the year.
- All material and labour costs are variable.
- Sales and distribution costs are variable in proportion to the turnover from each factory.
- Administration costs are fixed.

The Managing Director has proposed closing Dandelion. The impact to Blossom's results will be as follows:

- Revenue would increase by 40%.
- Fixed production overheads will increase by £100,000.
- Administration costs will increase by £60,000.
- It is forecast that raw material purchasing costs will decrease by 5% as a result of the closure.

(a) Prepare a revised statement of profit or loss for Blossom, assuming Dandelion is closed.

	Blossom £000	
Revenue		
Materials		
Direct labour		
Fixed production overheads		
Cost of sales		
Gross profit		%
Sales and distribution costs		
Administration costs		
Profit from operations		%

(b) Recommend whether Dandelion should be closed or remain open; give brief reasons for your answer.

(c) Give ONE example of a non-financial consideration which the Board of Directors of Daisy Ltd should consider prior to making their decision. State a potential problem for the company relating to this consideration.

Task 3.16

Connolly Computers Ltd (CCL) develops and licences specialist computer software and hardware. CCL is experiencing increasing competition from rival companies, most of which specialise in hardware or software, but not both. There is pressure to advertise and to cut prices.

You have been provided with the following information:

Statement of profit and loss

	Year ended 31 Dec 20X3 £000	20X2 £000
Revenue	15,206	13,524
Cost of sales	3,009	3,007
Gross profit	12,197	10,517
Distribution costs	3,006	1,996
Administrative expenses	994	1,768
Selling expenses	3,002	274
Profit from operations	5,195	6,479
Net interest receivable	995	395
Profit before tax	6,190	6,874
Income tax expense	3,104	1,452
Net profit	3,086	5,422

	Year ended 31 Dec 20X3 £000	20X2 £000
Retained profits	1,617	3,983
Dividends paid	1,469	1,439
	%	%
Accounting ratios and percentages		
Gross profit percentage	80	78
Expenses as a percentage of revenue		
Distribution costs	20	15
Administrative expenses	7	13
Selling expenses	20	2
Operating profit	34	48

The following information is also available:

- In order to try and compete with their rivals, a new e-commerce portal to allow retail customers to buy direct from CCL was built at a cost of £350,000. This was launched in October 20X3.
- The Managing Director decided at the start of 20X3 to focus on sales, and made redundancies, mainly in the financial and customer support areas. New staff were recruited in the warehouse and sales teams; they were brought in quickly and told to 'go out and sell'.
- Budgets are drawn up once a year, and actuals are compared to budget. CCL does not flex its budgets once approved.
- The tax rate remains static year on year.

(a) Evaluate whether the staff changes at CCL during 20X3 would have impacted upon the performance of the company. Identify any potential issues which may have arisen.

(b) Comment briefly on the financial performance of the company for the two years.

Task 3.17

Bradley Ltd manufactures two types of coffee machine, the X84 and Y78, which it manufactures in bulk for supermarkets and other retailers. The company has annual fixed overheads of £735,000 of which £488,000 relates to machine use, £85,000 to production set-ups and the balance to handling of orders.

The company expects the following activity in the next year:

	X84	Y78
Quantity made	12,000	25,000
Direct labour hours per unit	2	1
Machine hours per unit	3	1
Total number of production set-ups	10	40
Total number of orders	16	20

Complete the table below to show the overhead amount absorbed by each unit of each product under activity-based costing (give your answer to 2 decimal places).

Overhead	Cost driver units	Cost driver rate	Overhead absorbed for X84	Overhead absorbed for Y78
		Total overhead by product		
		Quantity made		
		Overhead absorbed per unit by product		

Task 3.18

Witney Ltd manufactures a single agricultural product at its factory and has the following results for its financial year:

	£'000
Sales	13,000
Direct material costs	(2,600)
Direct labour costs	(1,300)
Fixed overheads	(1,000)
Net profit	**8,100**

Production for the year was 130,000 units.

The company has performed an activity-based costing exercise and has traced its overheads to the following cost pools:

Cost pool	% of total overhead	Cost driver	Activity level
Order processing	25%	Orders processed	50,000
Sales force salaries	40%	Sales force hours worked	20,000
Research and development	35%	Department hours worked	10,000

Customer X66 made 400 orders during the year, required 300 hours of sales force time, 100 hours of research and purchased 1,000 units during the year.

Calculate the profit attributable to Customer X66 under activity-based costing.

Task 3.19

Conroy Ltd manufactures three products, K51, L18 and G14. Forecast statements of profit or loss for next year are as follows:

	K51 £'000	L18 £'000	G14 £'000	Total £'000
Sales	600	300	200	1,100
Cost of production:				
Materials	(200)	(60)	(30)	(290)
Labour	(95)	(20)	(10)	(125)
Variable overhead	(75)	(10)	(5)	(90)
Fixed overhead	(200)	(50)	(80)	(330)
Gross margin	**30**	**160**	**75**	**265**
Selling costs	(40)	(20)	(15)	(75)
Net margin	**(10)**	**140**	**60**	**190**

The directors are considering the closure of the K51 product line, due to the losses they anticipate will be incurred. You obtain the following information:

- Fixed production overheads consist of an apportionment of general factory overheads, based on 80% of direct materials cost. The remaining overheads are specific to the product concerned.
- Selling costs are based on commission paid to sales staff.

Should the K51 product line be shut down? (Yes/No)

Task 3.20

Leftfield Ltd manufactures four products and the profits currently earned by each are summarised below:

£	V1	R2	C3	M4	Total
Sales	75,000	60,000	30,000	25,000	190,000
Materials	(20,000)	(15,000)	(10,000)	(10,000)	(55,000)
Labour	(18,000)	(17,000)	(8,000)	(6,000)	(49,000)
Variable overheads	(9,000)	(8,500)	(4,000)	(3,000)	(24,500)
Contribution	**28,000**	**19,500**	**8,000**	**6,000**	**61,500**
Fixed costs	(15,000)	(11,250)	(7,500)	(7,500)	(41,250)
Profit/(loss)	**13,000**	**8,250**	**500**	**(1,500)**	**20,250**

The board of Leftfield Ltd is considering a proposal to shut down the manufacture of Product M4 in favour of a newly developed product. The fixed costs directly attributable to Product M4 are £2,500.

Forecast profits of the newly developed product are anticipated to be as follows:

£	New product
Sales	35,000
Materials	(15,000)
Labour	(4,000)
Variable overheads	(4,000)
Contribution	**12,000**
Fixed costs	(10,000)
Profit/(loss)	**2,000**

The directly attributable costs of the newly developed product are currently anticipated to be £8,000, although this figure might need to change depending on the results of the next round of product testing carried out. The newly developed product will also require the recruitment of a specialist quality control expert, although it is currently unclear whether this post could be filled from existing spare capacity.

Using the information supplied, determine whether the company should replace Product M4 with the newly developed product. You should consider whether there are any non-financial factors that might be relevant to this decision.

Task 3.21

Digital Ltd is a medium sized manufacturing company which produces two types of digital sports watches – the tracker and the tracker plus. The company has invested in new integrated technologies throughout all sections of the business, from the use of robotics in the production line, through to reporting software in the accounting function. A traditional absorption costing method is currently used and it has been suggested that activity-based costing may be more appropriate following the introduction of the new technology throughout the company.

The following information has been provided:

Product	Tracker	Tracker plus
Budgeted production units	50,000	20,000
Direct material per unit	£40	£50
Direct labour hours per unit @ £10 per hour	2	3
Number of inspections	290	110
IT support (hours)	5,000	15,000

The company has the following budgeted overheads:

	£
Inspections	100,000
IT support	140,000

(a) Calculate the direct costs and production overheads per unit for each product using the traditional direct labour hours absorption method.

	Tracker £	Tracker plus £
Direct cost		
Production overhead		
Total cost		

(b) Calculate the inspections and IT support costs per unit for each product using the activity-based costing method.

Enter your answers to two decimal places.

	Tracker £	Tracker plus £
Direct costs		
Inspection		
IT support		
Total cost		

(c) Discuss the differences between the product costs calculated using the traditional absorption costing method and activity-based costing method.

(d) Explain the benefits that the activity-based costing system may have over the traditional absorption costing method.

(e) Explain how the use of technology can provide benefit to Digital Ltd's operational control process.

Task 3.22

Service Ltd is considering closing its poor performing division, Advice, at the end of the financial year. You have collected the following information:

	Advice £	Help £	Total £
Sales revenue	50,000	180,000	230,000
Variable labour cost	(20,000)	(85,000)	(105,000)
Contribution	30,000	95,000	125,000
Fixed operating costs	(40,000)	(40,000)	(80,000)
Profit/(Loss)	(10,000)	55,000	45,000

Note 25% of the fixed operating costs relate to the specific division. The balance is an allocation of fixed head office overheads.

If a decision is made solely on the basis of relevant cost considerations, should Service Ltd close the Advice division?

▼

Picklist:

Yes
No

Chapter 4 – Ratio analysis

Task 4.1

Which of the following is the correct calculation of the working capital cycle?

	✓
Receivables days + Inventory days – Payables days	
Receivables days + Payables days – Inventory days	
Inventory days + Receivables days + Payables days	
Inventory days – Receivables days – Payables days	

Task 4.2

In accordance with the IASB Conceptual Framework for Financial Reporting:

(a) Identify the TWO fundamental characteristics of useful information.

	✓
Understandability	
Relevance	
Comparability	
Faithful representation	

(b) Define the term 'income'.

Task 4.3

You have been given the financial statements of Bridport Ltd for the year ending 30 June 20X1. You are now required to prepare financial ratios to assist your manager in his analysis of the company.

Bridport Ltd's statement of profit or loss and statement of financial position are shown below.

Bridport Ltd – Statement of profit or loss for the year ended 30 June 20X1

	£000
Continuing operations	
Revenue	58,914
Cost of sales	(42,126)
Gross profit	16,788
Distribution costs	(2,483)
Administrative expenses	(5,769)
Profit from operations	8,536
Finance costs	(1,642)
Profit before tax	6,894
Tax	(1,758)
Profit for the year from continuing operations	5,136

Bridport Ltd – Statement of financial position as at 30 June 20X1

	£000
ASSETS	
Non-current assets	
Property, plant and equipment	42,792
Current assets	
Inventories	6,724
Trade receivables	5,278
Cash and cash equivalents	1,190
	13,192
Total assets	55,984
EQUITY AND LIABILITIES	
Equity	
Ordinary share capital (£1 shares)	16,000
Retained earnings	12,326
Total equity	28,326

	£000
Non-current liabilities	
Bank loans	20,400
	20,400
Current liabilities	
Trade payables	5,332
Tax liabilities	1,926
	7,258
Total liabilities	27,658
Total equity and liabilities	55,984

(a) Identify the formulae that are used to calculate each of the following ratios:

Return on equity ▼

Picklist:

Profit after tax/Total equity × 100
Profit after tax/Total equity and liabilities × 100
Profit from operations/Total equity × 100
Profit from operations/Total equity and liabilities × 100

Acid test ratio ▼

Picklist:

(Current assets – Inventories)/Current liabilities
Current assets/Current liabilities
Non-current liabilities/(Total equity + Non-current liabilities)
Total assets/Total liabilities

Inventory holding period ▼

Picklist:

Cost of sales/Inventories
Inventories/Cost of sales × 365
Inventories/Revenue × 365
Revenue/Inventories

Asset turnover (net assets) ▼

Picklist:

Profit from operations/(Total assets – Current liabilities)
Profit from operations/Total assets
Revenue/(Total assets – Current liabilities)
Revenue/Total assets

Gearing ▼

Picklist:

Current assets/Current liabilities × 100
Non-current liabilities/(Total equity + Non-current liabilities) × 100
Profit from operations/(Total equity + Non-current liabilities) × 100
Revenue/(Total assets – Current liabilities) × 100

(b) Calculate the above ratios to ONE decimal place

Return on equity	☐	%
Acid test ratio	☐	: 1
Inventory holding period	☐	days
Asset turnover (net assets)	☐	times
Gearing	☐	%

Task 4.4

Carol Bright, the Financial Director of Poole Ltd, is concerned that the company is not managing its working capital efficiently. She has asked for your assistance in identifying any problem area(s) and for your suggestions as to how these can be remedied.

You have calculated the following ratios in respect of Poole Ltd's latest financial statements and have also obtained each of their industry averages for comparative purposes.

	Poole Ltd	Industry average
Current ratio	5.1:1	2.3:1
Inventory turnover	7.2 times	6.8 times
Trade receivables collection period	63 days	45 days
Trade payables payment period	44 days	51 days

Prepare a reply to Carol that includes:

(a) Comments on whether Poole Ltd has performed better or worse in respect of the calculated ratios, giving possible reasons, as compared to the industry averages.

(b) The steps to be taken to improve Poole Ltd's working capital cycle and any possible problems you think may arise from implementing these actions.

Task 4.5

Abbas Ltd uses a balanced scorecard to measure and control its financial performance. The Finance Director has asked you to calculate certain ratios for inclusion in the scorecard.

The following data is available.

Extracts from accounts of Abbas Ltd	Year ended 31 December 20X4 £000	Year ended 31 December 20X5 £000
Revenue	16,500	17,120
Cost of sales	7,540	8,480
Gross profit	8,960	8,640
Profit from operations	2,060	2,150
Assets		
Non-current assets	5,780	5,060
Inventories	2,450	2,900
Trade receivables	1,870	2,010
Cash and equivalents	30	340
Total assets	**10,130**	**10,310**
Equity and liabilities		
Equity	6,020	7,190
Non-current liabilities	2,590	1,070
Trade payables	1,130	1,670
Tax liabilities	390	380
Total equity and liabilities	**10,130**	**10,310**

(a) Which TWO of the following statements are recommended perspectives in the Balanced Scorecard framework?

	✓
Financial perspectives of the company, such as profit margins	
Supplier perspectives, such as the number of supplier complaints	
Customer perspectives of the company, such as number of repeat orders	

(b) Complete the Balanced Scorecard by calculating the ratios for the year ended 31 December 20X5. Answers should be rounded to ONE decimal point, or whole days.

Abbas Ltd Balanced Scorecard	Year ended 31 Dec 20X4	Year ended 31 Dec 20X5
Profitability and gearing (correct to 1 dp):		
Gross profit %	54.3%	%
Operating profit %	12.5%	%
Return on capital employed	23.9%	%
Gearing (debt/debt + equity)	30.1%	%
Liquidity ratios (correct to 1 dp):		
Current ratio	2.9:1	:1
Acid test/quick ratio	1.3:1	:1
Working capital days (correct to nearest day):		
Inventory holding period	119 days	days
Trade receivables collection period	41 days	days
Trade payables payment period	55 days	days
Working capital cycle	105 days	days

(c) Select the ONE correct observation about each aspect of business performance below.

(i) Profitability

	✓
This has been a year of steady, if unspectacular, progress. Although profitability has dipped, the return on capital employed has been kept under control.	
The profitability ratios give cause for concern. The small increase in sales revenue has not improved the gross profit percentage. Operating expenses have increased, reducing operating profit and return on capital employed.	
The ratios give mixed messages. Some have improved and some have deteriorated. Further investigation is required.	

(ii) Gearing

	✓
The decreased gearing ratio is due to the repayment of non-current liabilities.	
It is likely that the interest cover ratio has decreased.	
The increased gearing ratio shows that the company has become more risky.	

(iii) Liquidity

	✓
Both ratios have deteriorated which indicates that the company is less solvent than last year; however, both ratios still fall within an acceptable level.	
Both ratios remain quite high, which may indicate that working capital is not being used effectively.	
Some liquidity ratios have improved and some have deteriorated. Further investigation is required to understand whether liquidity is improving.	

(iv) Working capital

	✓
The working capital cycle has worsened. The inventory holding period has improved but the other ratios indicate a lack of financial control.	
There is a welcome improvement in the working capital cycle, mainly due to the change in the payment period for payables.	
The working capital cycle is worse than a year ago because of the increased revenue.	

(v) Overall performance

	✓
Profitability has declined in 20X5. However, the gearing and liquidity measures show an improving financial position.	
20X5 has been a bad year. Profitability has declined and finances are coming under pressure.	
Steady progress has been made in 20X5. The ratios show that the company is being better managed.	

Task 4.6

Explain the possible reasons for the following changes in the ratios of a company from one year to the next:

- **An increase in the current ratio**
- **A decrease in the gross profit margin**
- **An increase in the inventory holding period**
- **An increase in gearing**

Note. You are not required to show the calculation of the ratios.

Task 4.7

Answer the following questions with respect to ratio analysis.

(a) An entity has an average gross profit margin of 23% and an average inventory turnover of 8 times, which is similar to the averages for the industry.

The entity is likely to be:

	✓
An architectural practice	
A supermarket	
An estate agent	
A manufacturer	

(b) Extracts from the financial statements of Taurus are as follows:

Statement of profit or loss	£000
Operating profit	230
Finance costs	(15)
Profit before tax	215
Income tax	(15)
Profit for the year	200

Statement of financial position	£000
Ordinary shares	2,000
Revaluation surplus	300
Retained earnings	1,200
	3,500
10% loan	1,000
Current liabilities	100
Total equity and liabilities	4,600

What is the return on capital employed?

	✓
5.1%	
4.7%	
6.6%	
6%	

(c) Managing the operating cycle is an important part of managing working capital in a company.

Which of the following will increase the length of a company's operating cycle?

	✓
Reducing the receivables collection period	
Reducing the inventory holding period	
Reducing the payables payment period	
Reducing time taken to produce goods	

(d) Analysis of the financial statements of Capricorn at 31 December 20X8 yields the following information.

Gross profit margin	30%
Current ratio	2.14
ROCE	16.3%
Asset turnover	4.19
Inventory turnover	13.9

What is the operating profit margin?

	✓
3.9%	
7.6%	
16.1%	
7.1%	

Task 4.8

Forrest Limited is considering an acquisition of either Peas Limited or Carrots Ltd, which both operate in the same industry. You have been provided with extracts from the financial statements of both companies for the year ended 31 December 20X7.

Statements of profit and loss for the year ended 31 December 20X7

	Peas £000	Carrots £000
Revenue	12,000	20,500
Cost of sales	(10,500)	(18,000)
Gross profit	1,500	2,500
Operating expenses	(240)	(500)
Finance costs	(210)	(600)
Profit before tax	1,050	1,400
Income tax expense	(150)	(400)
Profit for the year	900	1,000
Note. Dividends paid during the year.	250	700

Statements of financial position as at 31 December 20X7

	Peas £000	Carrots £000
Non-current assets		
Freehold factory	2,600	Nil
Plant and machinery	5,000	7,400
	7,600	7,400
Current assets		
Inventory	2,000	3,600
Trade receivables	2,400	3,700
Bank	600	Nil
	5,000	7,300
Total assets	**12,600**	**14,700**
Equity and liabilities		
Equity shares of £1 each	2,000	2,000
Revaluation reserve	900	Nil
Retained earnings	2,600	800
	5,500	2,800
Non-current liabilities		
7% loan notes	3,000	3,200
10% loan notes	Nil	3,000
	3,000	6,200
Current liabilities		
Bank overdraft	Nil	1,700
Trade payables	3,100	3,800
Government grants	400	Nil
Taxation	600	200
	4,100	5,700
Total equity and liabilities	**12,600**	**14,700**

(a) Calculate the following ratios for both companies, rounding off to ONE decimal place, or the nearest whole day:

	Peas	Carrots
Return on year-end capital employed (ROCE)		
Gross profit margin		
Operating profit margin		
Current ratio		
Closing inventory holding period		
Trade receivables' collection period		
Trade payables' payment period		
Gearing		
Interest cover		
Dividend cover		

(b) Critically appraise the relative performance and financial position of Peas and Carrots for the year ended 31 December 20X7, in light of the potential acquisition by Forrest.

Profitability

Gearing

Liquidity

Summary

Task 4.9

The most recent financial statements of Tiger Tea plc (TTP) are shown below:

Statements of profit or loss for the year ended 31 December

	20X1 £000	20X0 £000
Revenue	25,500	17,250
Cost of sales	(14,800)	(10,350)
Gross profit	10,700	6,900
Distribution costs	(2,700)	(1,850)
Administrative expenses	(2,100)	(1,450)
Profit from operations	5,900	3,600
Finance costs	(650)	(100)
Profit before taxation	5,250	3,500
Income tax expense	(2,250)	(1,000)
Profit for the year	3,000	2,500

Statements of financial position as at 31 December

	20X1 £000	20X0 £000
ASSETS		
Non-current assets		
Property, plant and equipment	11,500	5,400
Intangibles	6,200	Nil
	17,700	5,400
Current assets		
Inventory	3,600	1,800
Trade receivables	2,400	1,400
Bank	Nil	4,000
	6,000	7,200
TOTAL ASSETS	**23,700**	**12,600**

	20X1 £000	20X0 £000
EQUITY AND LIABILITIES		
Equity		
Equity shares of £1 each	5,000	5,000
Retained earnings	4,500	2,250
	9,500	7,250
Non-current liabilities		
5% loan notes	2,000	2,000
8% loan notes	7,000	Nil
	9,000	2,000
Current liabilities		
Bank overdraft	200	Nil
Trade payables	2,800	2,150
Current tax payable	2,200	1,200
	5,200	3,350
TOTAL EQUITY AND LIABILITIES	**23,700**	**12,600**

(a) Calculate the following ratios for each year, rounding off to ONE decimal place, or the nearest day.

	20X1	20X0
Net profit %		
Operating profit %		
Gross profit %		
ROCE		
ROE		
Gearing		
Interest cover		
Current ratio		
Quick ratio		

(b) Critically comment on the performance in 20X1 relative to 20X0 from the perspective of shareholders, under the following headings:

Profitability

Gearing

Liquidity

Chapter 5 – Internal controls

Task 5.1

To date Rees Ltd has paid its suppliers by cheque. Rees Ltd now plans to pay larger suppliers by BACS, extending this method to all suppliers in time.

Complete the following statements.

Rees Ltd's plan is [▼] change.

Picklist:

a transformational
an incremental

The fact that the time of Rees Ltd's accounting staff will be freed up by not having to complete cheques by hand is [▼] .

Picklist:

a tangible benefit of the change
a tangible cost of the change
an intangible benefit of the change
an intangible cost of the change

Task 5.2

You have been asked to identify some improvements to the controls in Sleeptight Ltd's sales ordering procedures.

- Sleeptight Ltd makes high-value bespoke wooden bedroom furniture to order.
- An official customer order is created for each sale by a sales executive. The order must state the product and agreed delivery date. It also states the approximate price.
- Customer orders must be reviewed and signed by the sales manager.
- Orders for more than three pieces of furniture for one customer must be signed by the sales director.

(a) Identify ONE strength in these procedures. Explain how the business benefits from this.

(b) Identify ONE weakness in these procedures. Explain how this damages the business and suggest a remedy.

(c) Identify an opportunity to improve the procedures. Explain how the procedure should be changed and how the business could benefit.

Task 5.3

You have been asked to suggest some improvements to the controls in Sleeptight Ltd's sales accounting procedures.

- Sleeptight Ltd makes high-value bespoke wooden bedroom furniture to order.
- The company operates an integrated accounting system which includes a sales accounting module. The sales manager is responsible for managing all sales activities.
- Before an order is taken from a new customer, the sales manager performs a credit check on them and obtains their banking details. The sales manager has the authority either to offer credit terms or to require payment by bank transfer before delivery of the furniture.
- Credit terms offered are always two months from the end of the month in which delivery takes place, with a 15% discount for payment within 10 days of delivery. Payment is required via bank transfer.
- All sales invoices are raised by the accounts receivable clerk, who produces the invoice by checking the despatch note to the customer order, then confirming the agreed price and terms with the sales manager.
- The accounts receivable clerk posts the invoices to the computerised accounting system, answers any queries from customers and issues credit notes when appropriate.
- The accounts receivable clerk checks the bank account weekly for bank transfers by customers and posts receipts to the ledger accounts.

(a) Identify ONE strength in these procedures. Explain how the business benefits from this.

(b) Identify ONE weakness in these procedures. Explain how this damages the business and suggest a remedy.

(c) Identify an opportunity to improve the procedures. Explain how the procedure should be changed and how the business could benefit.

Task 5.4

You have been asked to suggest some improvements to the controls in Sleeptight Ltd's purchase ordering procedures.

- Sleeptight Ltd makes high-value bespoke wooden bedroom furniture to order.
- All purchases, except petty cash items, must be documented on an official purchase order. The order should state the agreed price, if known.
- All departments are provided with books of pre-numbered order forms. These books can be obtained from the stationery store.
- Orders for production materials must be signed by the production manager.
- Capital expenditure orders must be signed by the finance director.
- There is no cash limit for purchase orders provided that they are within the approved budget.
- Other orders must be signed by the relevant budget holders.
- New suppliers are given a trade reference by the purchasing manager, who also requests credit terms. These are subject to negotiation, though the company's preferred terms are to pay 60 days from the end of the month in which delivery takes place.

(a) Identify ONE strength in these procedures. Explain how the business benefits from this.

(b) Identify the weaknesses in these procedures. Explain how each one damages the business and suggest a remedy.

(c) Identify an opportunity to improve the procedures. Explain how the procedure should be changed and how the business could benefit.

Task 5.5

You have been asked to suggest some improvements to the controls in Sleeptight Ltd's purchase accounting procedures.

- Sleeptight Ltd makes high-value bespoke wooden bedroom furniture to order.
- Four copies of each purchase order form are printed. Once signed, the original is sent to the supplier. A yellow copy is sent to the accounts payable clerk. A pink copy is retained by the individual who raised the order, while a green copy is sent to Goods Inwards.
- When the goods or service(s) are received, Goods Inwards checks the goods, signs the green copy and sends it to the accounts payable clerk.
- All purchase invoices received are checked by the accounts payable clerk, who checks the calculations, matches them to appropriate yellow and signed green copy orders and clears the invoices for payment.
- The accounts payable clerk posts the cleared invoices to the computerised accounting system and takes up queries with suppliers, requesting credit notes when appropriate.
- Invoices are automatically paid as they fall due through the bankers automated clearing system (BACS). The accounts payable clerk authorises one payment run every week.
- The accounts payable clerk is authorised to pay early if a discount of at least 5% is offered by the supplier.

(a) Identify the strengths in these procedures. Explain how the business benefits from these.

(b) Identify ONE weakness in these procedures. Explain how this damages the business and suggest a remedy.

Task 5.6

You have been asked to review the adequacy of the control in Sleeptight Ltd's payroll procedures.

The company operates an integrated accounting system which includes a payroll accounting module. The accounts manager, based at the head office, is responsible for managing payroll activities. The payroll clerk, based at the factory, performs day-to-day payroll tasks.

- Sleeptight Ltd makes high-value bespoke wooden bedroom furniture to order.
- Non-production staff are salaried and are not entitled to paid overtime.
- Production staff are all full-time. They are paid at time and a half their basic rate if they work more than 40 hours per week.
- Production staff sign themselves in and out of the factory each day, using the signing-in book which is kept in the staff locker room.
- Production staff record hours spent on individual items of bespoke furniture on job sheets that follow the items around the factory. These job sheets are checked and signed by production supervisors.

The payroll clerk:

- Maintains standing data on employees
- Calculates each employee's hours at work each week from the signing-in book
- Calculates gross pay and deductions for production staff weekly, and for other staff monthly
- Maintains the wages control account
- Prepares the bank payments each week/month to employees and HMRC
- Reconciles total pay and deductions in the wages control account

Once a month the accounts manager reviews total payroll cost against budget and investigates any large unexpected variances.

(a) Identify ONE strength in these procedures. Explain how the business benefits from this.

(b) Identify the weaknesses in these procedures. Explain how these damage the business and suggest remedies.

(c) Identify an opportunity to improve the procedures. Explain how the procedure should be changed and how the business could benefit.

Task 5.7

A company wishes to avoid or reduce certain specific risks in each of its three main transaction streams.

You are required to identify a control objective and control activity for each risk.

Transaction stream	Risk	Control objective	Control activity
Purchasing	Company pays for goods it does not receive		
Sales	Sales recorded late so fines incurred from HMRC with respect to VAT		
Payroll	Company overpays		

Task 5.8

You are presented with the monthly operating report below. The original budget has been flexed to the level of actual activity, and variances calculated.

You are told that:

- Material, labour and distribution costs are variable.
- Energy cost is semi-variable. The fixed element is budgeted at £12,800 per month.
- Equipment hire is a stepped cost, budgeted to increase at every 30,000 units of monthly production.
- Depreciation, marketing and administration costs are fixed.
- The company does not use full absorption costing.

Monthly operating report

Original budget		Flexed budget	Actual	Variance Fav/(Adv)
178,000	Sales volume (units)		192,000	
£		£	£	£
1,281,600	Sales revenue	1,382,400	1,377,000	–5,400
	Costs			
462,800	Materials	499,200	500,100	–900
480,600	Labour	518,400	516,500	1,900
67,640	Distribution	72,960	74,200	–1,240
60,860	Energy	64,640	65,080	–440
24,000	Equipment hire	28,000	28,600	–600
8,800	Depreciation	8,800	8,700	100
78,000	Marketing	78,000	78,900	–900
25,600	Administration	25,600	24,820	780
1,208,300	Total	1,295,600	1,296,900	–1,300
73,300	Operating profit/(loss)	86,800	80,100	–6,700

Write an email to the chief executive to explain the following.

(a) The main factors that led to the actual profit being higher than the original budgeted profit.

(b) Whether improved internal controls might assist in controlling the adverse variances.

Task 5.9

A company wishes to avoid or reduce certain specific risks in each of its three main transaction streams.

You are required to identify a control objective and control activity for each risk.

Transaction stream	Risk	Control objective	Control activity
Payroll	Company incurs fines from HMRC		
Sales	Custom lost through chasing payments already made by the customer		
Purchasing	Company pays the wrong supplier		

Task 5.10

A firm of accountants, Crachett & Co has decided to train all new staff in basic bookkeeping as part of their induction programme.

(a) Identify the costs of such a decision, explaining the terms 'tangible costs' and 'intangible costs' in your response.

As part of the reorganisation of the firm of accountants, other areas of the business are being reviewed. Crachett & Co are also considering a new accountancy software; however, it is expensive and the partners are unsure about whether to commit to it.

A software company, MoneyWise has quoted Crachett & Co for their new system.

Dear Accountants,

Thank you for your interest in our fully integrated Client Pro Systems accounting system. We are happy to provide you with details of the following:

- Client Pro System 1 (Cloud).
- Sales ledger system, including pre-numbered invoices and aged debt reports.
- Purchases ledger system, incorporating purchase orders which can be matched against incoming invoices. Inventory aging reports are included.
- General ledger and summary trial balance reports.
- Exception reporting.
- Financial reporting tool for multi-client usage, incorporating iXBRL tax information, bookkeeping interface and payroll facility.
- Updates and upgrades occur regularly and will be automated at no extra cost.

Annual costs

	Initial costs	Annual costs
Client Pro system 1 (cloud)	£7,500 (to cover assistance with data migration)	£3,300 (up to 15 licensed users)

Training costs for the new system would be:

In-house training (maximum of 15 people)	£2,700
Course at local college (1 day)	£275 per person
Online course (completed in own time)	£75 per person (access limited to 6 months)

If you have any further questions, please do not hesitate to contact us.

Yours sincerely

E.Scrooge

Sales Director
MoneyWise

(b) Evaluate the proposed new software, considering the factors in a cost-benefit analysis.

Answer Bank

Chapter 1 – The accounting function

Task 1.1

(a) If you want your accounting system to be integrated then you need to [centralise it].

A key benefit of integrating the company's accounting system is that you can ensure every area of the business complies with relevant [laws and regulations].

(b)

Criterion	Centralised accounting function ✓	Decentralised accounting function ✓
More economies of scope	✓	
Better communication with business units		✓
Better placed to produce group accounts	✓	
More economies of scale	✓	

Task 1.2

Task	Responsible party
Preparation of budgetary control reports	Management accountant
Maintain accounting ledgers	Financial accountant
Cash management	Treasury manager

Task 1.3

Party	Responsibility
External auditors	Report whether the financial statements show a true and fair view
Accounting function	Maintain the accounting system
Directors	Prepare financial statements for the company

Task 1.4

(a)

	✓
Professional behaviour	
Objectivity	
Professional competence and due care	✓
Integrity	

(b)

Confidentiality

She must refuse to reveal the information and decline the trip

Task 1.5

(a)

Control activity	Type of control
Securing invoices in a locked cupboard	Physical control
Authorising changes to standing data	Integrity control

(b)

	✓
Mmmeee	
82s09PQ#	✓
1357abcd	

Task 1.6

	✓
Reverse the duplicate entries and advise the sales ledger team of his action	
Inform the sales invoicing team of the error	✓
Report the error to the chief accountant	
Prepare a credit note and send it to the customer	

Task 1.7

Error	Detected by reconciliation?
A batch of purchase invoices posted to the sales ledger control account	Yes
A pricing error in a sales invoice	No
VAT on a sales invoice posted to insurance rather than the VAT control account	No
A sales invoice posted to the wrong customer account	No
A sales invoice credited to the customer's account	Yes

Task 1.8

The proposed action violates the principle of segregation of duties. This means that different people should be responsible for different parts of the accounting system to minimise the chance of fraud and error.

For example, if Iqbal were to perform all of these functions he could potentially steal cash received from a customer and cover it up by writing off the debt or issuing a credit note.

If Iqbal were to make errors in performing his duties, for example issuing the same invoice twice (as in Task 1.6), then the chances of it being detected are reduced if there are no other people involved. It is much easier to spot errors made by other people than to spot your own.

Finally, Iqbal could well become overburdened by his increased responsibilities. This is likely to lead to more errors and also a lack of efficiency in, for example, chasing customers for payment.

Task 1.9

Mission statements are published for the benefit of employees and other stakeholders of the organisation, such as the customers and suppliers. There is no standard format, but mission statements should generally be:

- **Brief** – to help ensure they are easy to understand and remember
- **Flexible** – to help accommodate change
- **Distinctive** – to make the organisation stand out

Mission statements are useful as they allow management to refer to the core beliefs of the business. This is especially important if the company is considering moving into new business areas, such as Star Supplies growing their own produce or delivering fast food. By considering the mission statement, management can see whether the new ideas are a 'good fit' for the current business, or whether it may only add to confusion for the existing customer and supplier base.

Task 1.10

Iqbal has breached the principle of confidentiality. He has gained information during the course of his employment and should not reveal that information to any unauthorised person, without the prior consent of all parties; nor should he use it for his own purposes.

Iqbal should not reveal the information to a third party and he should also not reveal the information to anyone within JSL who does not require the information by virtue of their duties. For example, it would be acceptable to reveal the information to the Chief Accountant but not to the payroll clerk.

Iqbal may also be considered to have breached the principle of professional behaviour, by spreading rumours about TL Ltd. Iqbal has no confirmed evidence that TL is, in fact, in financial difficulty.

Task 1.11

	✓
A discussion of sales figures for the main three products of JSL	
Highlighting the employee volunteering opportunities from a team helping to re-turf a school football pitch	✓
Reporting on the recycling efforts within the office environment	✓
Reporting any incidents of money laundering and how the organisation seeks to change its controls going forward	✓

A sustainability report will look at any non-compliance with regulations (money laundering), any organisational efforts to reduce the environmental impact (recycling) and raising awareness of social responsibility (helping out a local school). The sales figures are more likely to be mentioned as part of performance within a director's report (if at all) to support any going concern worries by stakeholders, or more likely, not to be mentioned in any great detail in public financial statements.

Task 1.12

	✓
It is a memorandum account to keep track of amounts owing from individual customers and owed to individual suppliers.	
It will detect all bookkeeping errors.	
It is prepared after closing off the general ledger accounts and before preparing the final accounts.	✓
It will always include a suspense account.	

The trial balance lists the closing balances on each general ledger account. The balances are listed on the debit or credit side as appropriate. It is an important step in the preparation of the final accounts.

It is not a memorandum account showing amounts owing from individual customers or owed to individual suppliers; this is a description of the subsidiary payables and receivables ledgers.

It will not detect every error as some errors allow the trial balance to balance.

It only includes a suspense account if it does not initially balance; it will not always include a suspense account.

Task 1.13

(a) | £ | 6,480 |

Working:

£32,400 (from the trial balance) × 20% = £6,480.

(b) Extract from the adjusted trial balance

Ledger account	Initial trial balance		Adjustments	
	Debit £	Credit £	Debit £	Credit £
Bank	5,321			**140**
Carriage outwards			**460**	
Depreciation charges			**6,480**	
Irrecoverable debts	632			
Office expenses	52,832		**140**	
Payables ledger control account		11,230		
Plant at cost	32,400			
Plant accumulated depreciation		6,480		**6,480**
Prepaid expenses	305			
Purchases	89,430			**890**
Receivables ledger control account	16,230			
Rent	12,520			
Sales		104,502		
Suspense		430	**890**	**460**
VAT		9,320		

Workings:

Offices expenses: £70 × 2 = £140

Purchases balance: £89,430 – £88,540 = £890

Chapter 2 – Accounting control systems and procedures

Task 2.1

Allocating a payment from one customer to another customer's account in order to balance the books and detract from a shortfall is called teeming and lading.

Task 2.2

	✓
False representation	✓
Failure to segregate duties	
Failure to disclose information	✓
Abuse of position	✓
Duress and undue influence	

Task 2.3

Systemic weakness	Understatement of reported profit ✓	Overstatement of reported profit ✓
Overvaluation of inventory at the period end		✓
Creating an unnecessary allowance for doubtful debts	✓	
Fictitious sales		✓
Not writing off irrecoverable debts		✓
Overstating expenses	✓	

Task 2.4

Systemic weakness	Misappropriation of assets ✓	Misstatement in the financial statements ✓
Leaving offices where computers are held unlocked	✓	
Failing to maintain an asset register		✓
Omitting inventory from the annual physical count		✓
Creating a fictitious employee on the payroll	✓	✓
Failing to chase unpaid debts		✓

Task 2.5

Segregation of duties is a type of staff control over fraud in the accounting system. This is because segregation of duties relates to staffing levels and responsibilities.

Task 2.6

No.	Weakness	Potential problem
1	The sales manager appears to have very little involvement in day to day sales, apart from negotiating terms with new customers.	Failures in the system and system abuses could go unnoticed.
2	The procedures do not include any mention of quality control checks ensuring that goods of the correct category and standard have been despatched.	If this is not happening the company could be sending out sub-standard goods.
3	Orders can be taken without agreeing a price.	The company is in a weak position to negotiate price after the goods have been despatched.
4	Despatch signs the green copy of the order, but there is no signed goods received note from the customer, confirming receipt of the goods.	Goods could be delivered to the wrong address, or not delivered at all and still charged for. This could cause problems with customer goodwill as well as creating potential for fraud.
5	Lack of authorisation of new accounts.	There should be a policy for deciding on whether to offer any credit at all. Potential for fraud through collusion with customers.
6	The terms agreed by the sales manager are not countersigned.	Potential for fraud through collusion with customers.
7	Only one signature is required on most orders.	Potential for fraud through collusion with customers.
8	The accounts receivable clerk checks, clears and arranges payment of invoices. She also handles customer queries, issues credit notes and records the receipt of payments. There is a lack of segregation of duties.	Potential for fraud through collusion with customers.
9	The sales manager and accounts receivable clerk control all aspects of sales accounting.	Potential for fraud through collusion.
10	Cash receipts are only monitored and posted once a week.	Increases the opportunity for teeming and lading, and means a bad service will be given to customers if they ring with a query.
11	No counter-signatory required for credit notes.	Potential for fraud through collusion with customers.

Task 2.7

	✓
Physical controls	
Segregation of duties	✓
Management controls	
Supervisory controls	✓
Organisation	
Authorisation (approval) of transactions	✓
Arithmetic and bookkeeping checks	
Personnel controls	

Task 2.8

Note. Other valid weaknesses may have been identified and would gain credit.

No.	Weakness	Potential problem
1	Only hand-written notes are made rather than a pre-numbered requisition form.	Requisition details might be lost and might not be followed up. As they are hand written, it could be difficult to read the writing and errors could be made.
2	Requisitions are not authorised.	Employees could order goods for their own use or that the business does not need.
3	Purchasing manager should obtain quotations from several suppliers.	The company could pay higher prices than necessary, hence wasting resources.
4	There is no system for recording receipt of other goods and services.	The company may pay for other goods and services which have not been received.
5	Invoices are only matched to purchase orders 'if they are available'. There is no mention of investigating missing purchase orders. No goods should be ordered without a valid purchase order.	The company could receive goods which have not been ordered, or are not authorised.
6	Purchases ledger clerk performs too many tasks.	There is increased chance of fraud or error.
7	Invoices are not authorised before being paid.	There is increased risk of fraud or error.

Task 2.9

Note. Other valid weaknesses may have been identified and would gain credit.

No.	Weakness	Potential problem
1	Blank timekeeping cards are used. These should be pre-printed with the employee name and number and should be pre-numbered.	Timekeeping cards could go missing.
2	There is no supervision over the signing in or signing out and no ID is required.	Employees could record fictitious hours and employees could sign in or out for their colleagues.
3	No independent personnel function.	Supervisors and wages clerk could add fictitious employees to the payroll and misappropriate their wages.
4	Lack of segregation of duties with the wages clerk.	The wages clerk could misappropriate funds.
5	No control over weekly payroll, such as reconciling it to the prior month's payroll.	Hours worked could be incorrectly entered.
6	Only one person banks the cheque, collects the cash and draws up the pay packets.	Cash cheque could be misappropriated either before reaching wages clerk or by the wages clerk.
7	The pay packets are not checked against the payroll and signed for by the supervisors when they take control of them.	Pay packets could be incorrect or could go missing, resulting in a loss of cash to the company (if the packets are too high) or disgruntled staff (if the packets are too low or if they are missing).
8	Employees do not count and sign for their pay packets and their IDs are not required.	Employees could claim not to have been paid, or could dispute the amount of their pay packets raising unpleasant disputes with the company, which could result in financial losses to the company.
9	Inadequate control over the distribution itself. There is only one supervisor present and it is not a formal process.	Supervisors could sign for absent or terminated employees and collect their wages.
10	No procedure for unclaimed wages.	Unclaimed wages could be misappropriated.
11	Poor control over hiring employees: job vacancies are not authorised, there is no mention of an interviewing process and no mention of authorising the employment contract.	Staff could be hired without the necessary references and qualifications. Unnecessary staff could be hired, and fictitious staff could be created and their pay misappropriated.
12	Verbal authorisation for pay increases.	Increases could be made that are not authorised, resulting in the misappropriation of funds, or resulting in a payroll that the company cannot afford.

Chapter 3 – Decision making and control

Task 3.1

The [fixed overheads] total variance may be analysed into expenditure, efficiency and capacity variances.

Task 3.2

Complete the following statements:

(a) The standard quantity of labour per unit is [15] minutes.

(b) The standard quantity of materials needed to produce 13,500 units of X07 is [16,875] litres.

(c) The standard labour hours to produce 12,000 units of X07 is [3,000] hours.

(d) The standard labour cost to produce 13,500 units of X07 is [£ 57,375]

(e) The standard overhead absorption rate per unit is [£ 5.50].

Workings

(a) 3,500 direct labour hours/14,000 units = 0.25 hours (15 minutes)

(b) Standard quantity per unit = 17,500 litres/14,000 units = 1.25 litres

13,500 units × 1.25 litres = 16,875 litres

(c) Standard labour hours per unit = 0.25 hours (see part (a))

12,000 units × 0.25 hours = 3,000 hours

(d) Standard labour cost per unit = £59,500/14,000 units = £4.25

13,500 units × £4.25 hours = £57,375

(e) Standard OAR = £77,000/14,000 units = £5.50 per unit

Task 3.3

(a)

The standard cost per kilogram is [£ 2.50].

Working

£10,915 – £1,665 = £9,250 standard cost

Standard cost per kilogram = £9,250/3,700 kilograms = £2.50

(b)

The material usage variance is [£ 6,000] [adverse].

Working

19,000 units should use (× 10 litres per unit)	190,000 litres
But did use	200,000 litres
Material usage variance in litres	10,000 litres (A)
× standard costs per litre (£132,000/ 220,000 litres)	× £0.60
Material usage variance in £	£6,000 (A)

(c)

The total labour efficiency variance is £ 4,500 favourable .

The idle time variance is £ 6,000 adverse .

Working

Labour efficiency variance

12,000 units should have taken (× 0.6 hours)	7,200 hrs
But did take	6,900 hrs
	300 hrs (F)
At standard rate	× £15.00
Efficiency variance	£4,500 (F)

Idle time variance

7,300 hours – 6,900 hours = 400 hours idle time

400 hours × £15.00 = £6,000 (A)

Task 3.4

The fixed overhead volume variance is £ 25,000 favourable

Working

	£
OAR is £350,000/28,000 = £12.50 per unit	
Actual production @ standard OAR 30,000 × £12.50	375,000
Budgeted production @ standard OAR 28,000 × £12.50	350,000
Volume variance	25,000 (F)

The actual fixed production overheads incurred were £ 315,000 .

Working

	£
Budgeted overhead	350,000
Actual overhead (Balancing figure)	315,000
Expenditure variance	35,000 (F)

Task 3.5

Variance	Amount £	Adverse/ Favourable
Fixed overhead capacity	448,000	favourable
Fixed overhead efficiency	268,000	adverse

Workings

Fixed overhead capacity variance

	£
OAR is £3,840,000/480,000 = £8.00 per labour hour	
Actual hours @ standard OAR 536,000 × £8.00	4,288,000
Budgeted hours @ standard OAR 480,000 × £8.00	3,840,000
Capacity variance	448,000 (F)

Fixed overhead efficiency variance

	£
Standard hours for actual production @ standard OAR 67,000 × 7.5 hours × £8.00	4,020,000
Actual hours @ standard OAR 536,000 × £8.00	4,288,000
Efficiency variance	268,000 (A)

Task 3.6

			£
Budgeted variable cost for actual production			387,600
Budgeted fixed cost			234,000
Total budgeted cost for actual production			621,600
Variance	**Favourable £**	**Adverse £**	
Direct materials price	18,700		
Direct materials usage	11,900		
Direct labour rate		28,560	
Direct labour efficiency		12,240	
Fixed overhead expenditure	13,000		
Fixed overhead volume	N/A	N/A	
Total variance	43,600	40,800	–2,800
Actual cost of actual production			618,800

Workings

Budgeted variable cost per unit = (£130,200 + £223,200)/12,400 units = £28.50

Budgeted variable cost for actual production = 13,600 units × £28.50 = £387,600

Total budgeted cost for actual production = £387,600 + £234,000 (fixed costs) = £621,600

Direct labour efficiency variance

13,600 units should have taken (× 2 hours)	27,200 hrs
But did take	28,560 hrs
	1,360 hrs (A)
At standard rate	× £9.00
Efficiency variance	£12,240 (A)

Fixed overhead expenditure variance = Actual £13,000 lower than budgeted, so favourable.

Task 3.7

(a) The part of the variance explained by the increase in the price index is

£	281,250 (A)

.

Working

	£
12,500 litres × £450 (original standard rate)	5,625,000
12,500 litres × £472.50 (£450 × 126.525/120.50)	5,906,250
	281,250 (A)

(b) The part of the variance not explained by the increase in the price index is

£	93,750

.

Working

£375,000 – £281,250 = £93,750

(c) The percentage increase in the index is [ ] %.

Working

(126.525 – 120.50)/120.50 = 0.05 (5%)

(d)

	September 20X3 £	December 20X3 £
Cost per kilogram of Z4QX	2,136.62	2,543.84

Workings

Difference between April 20X3 and May 20X3 = £135.74

Difference between May 20X3 and June 20X3 = £135.74

September 20X3 cost = £1,729.40 (June 20X3) + (£135.74 × 3) = £2,136.62

December 20X3 cost = £2,136.62 (September X3) + (£135.74 × 3) = £2,543.84

(e) The forecast cost per kilogram, using the regression line, for September 20X3 is

£	118.85

Workings

June 20X3 is period 41. Therefore September 20X3 = period 44.

y = 24.69 + 2.14x   where y = cost per kilogram   x = the period

y = 24.69 + (2.14 × 44)

y = £118.85

Task 3.8

Total direct material variance

The total direct material variance simply compares the **flexed budget** for materials with the actual cost incurred. The flexed budget is the total budgeted cost of materials for the actual production; 21,000 units in this example. It is incorrect to calculate the variance as £74,500 adverse by comparing the actual cost of £954,500 with the original budgeted cost of £880,000.

The flexing of the budget calculates the **quantity of materials** which are expected to be used to produce the **actual production**. Therefore, the expected usage of materials to produce 21,000 units is £924,000 (if 80,000 kilograms costing £880,000 is required to make 20,000 units then it follows, assuming that the material cost and quantity is perfectly variable, that to make 21,000 units requires 84,000 kilograms at a cost of £11 per kilogram (£880,000/80,000)).

This flexed budget can now be **compared with the actual** costs to produce the total material variance of £30,500. This variance is adverse because the **actual cost was greater than the flexed budgeted cost**.

This total variance can now be split into two elements:

- The variance due to the price being different from that which was expected: the material price variance.
- The variance due to the quantity of material used per unit of production being different from that which was expected: the material usage variance.

The expected (standard or budgeted or planned) price is £11 per kilogram (£880,000/80,000) and therefore the expected cost of 83,000 kilograms must be 83,000 kilograms at £11 per kilogram. This is £913,000.

The price variance can now be calculated by taking the actual cost (price paid) for the 83,000 kilograms and comparing this to the expected cost. This results in £913,000, compared to £954,500: a variance of £41,500. This variance is adverse because the **actual cost is greater than the expected cost**.

The material usage variance is calculated by taking the quantity of materials which would be expected to be used to produce the actual volume of production. In this case 21,000 units were produced and the expected quantity of materials for each unit is 4 kilograms (80,000 kilograms/20,000 units). Therefore, to produce 21,000 units requires 84,000 kilograms of material. Compare this with the actual quantity used of 83,000 kilograms produces a variance of 1,000 kilograms. This is favourable and needs to be **valued at the expected cost** of £11 per kilogram, giving £11,000.

The usage variance is always **valued at the standard cost** (expected/planned or budgeted) because the price variance has already been isolated. If both variances have been calculated correctly they should reconcile back to the total materials variance. In this example, the price variance of £41,500 adverse less the £11,000 favourable usage variance is reconciled to the total variance of £30,500 adverse.

Task 3.9

(a)

	Scenario 1	Scenario 2
Return on capital employed	11.96%	9.52%
Inventory holding period in days	50.00	45.29
Sales price per unit	£14.00	£12.00
Full production cost per unit	£9.00	£9.00

Workings

Return on capital employed
Scenario 1 = £275,000/£2,298,400 × 100% = 11.96%
Scenario 2 = £200,000/£2,100,340 × 100% = 9.52%

Inventory holding period
Scenario 1 = £147,950/(£1,680,000 – £600,000) × 365 = 50.00 days
Scenario 2 = £167,500/(£1,800,000 – £450,000) × 365 = 45.29 days

Sales price per unit
Scenario 1 = £1,680,000/120,000 = £14.00
Scenario 2 = £1,800,000/150,000 = £12.00

Full production cost per unit
Scenario 1 = (£1,680,000 – £600,000)/120,000 = £9.00
Scenario 2 = (£1,800,000 – £450,000)/150,000 = £9.00

(b)

	Scenario 3
Capital employed (£)	175,000
Return on capital employed (%)	13
Profit margin (%)	14
Gearing (%)	32.75
Profit (to the nearest £)	22,750
Sales revenue (to the nearest £)	162,500

Workings

Profit (to the nearest £) = £175,000 × (13/100) = £22,750

Sales revenue (to the nearest £) = £22,750 ÷ (14/100) = £162,500

(c)

Total non-current liabilities			
———	×	100	
Total equity			

Or

Total non-current liabilities			
———	×	100	
Total non-current liabilities plus Total equity			

Task 3.10

(a)

	Product Tig £	Product Tag £
The contribution per unit is	1,200	1,350
The contribution per kilogram of materials is	200	180

Workings

Contribution per unit

Product Tig = £4,000 – £2,800 = £1,200
Product Tag = £4,950 – £3,600 = £1,350

Contribution per kilogram of material

Product Tig = £1,200/6 kg = £200
Product Tag = £1,350/7.5 kg = £180

(b) The optimal production order for products Tig and Tag is Tig then Tag.

(Based on the contribution per kilogram of material calculated in part (a)).

(c)

	Product Tig	Product Tag
Production in units	200	240

Workings

Supply is limited to 3,000 kilograms of material

Product Tig then Tag (based on part (b))

200 units of Tig × 6 kg per unit = 1,200 kg (so 1,800 kg remaining to produce Tag)

1,800 kg/7.5 kg per unit = 240 units of Tag

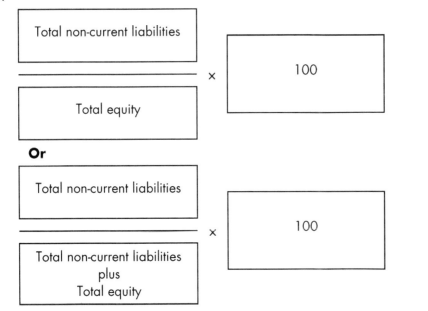

(d)

	Product Tig £	Product Tag £
Total contribution	240,000	324,000

Workings

Product Tig = 200 units × £1,200 = £240,000
Product Tag = 240 units × £1,350 = £324,000

(e)

Should Alpha Ltd purchase the additional material?	Give a reason
(1) Yes	**(2)** The additional cost per kilogram is less than the contribution per kilogram.

Task 3.11

(a)

	Sales price £40	Sales price £50
The target total production cost per unit	£28	£35
The target fixed production cost per unit	£16	£22
The target total fixed production cost	£8,000,000	£9,460,000

Workings

Target total production cost per unit
Sales price £40 = £40 × 70/100 = £28
Sales price £50 = £50 × 70/100 = £35

Target fixed production cost per unit
Sales price £40 = £28 – £12 = £16
Sales price £50 = £35 – £13 = £22

Target fixed production cost
Sales price £40 = £16 per unit × 500,000 = £8,000,000
Sales price £50 = £22 per unit × 430,000 = £9,460,000

(b) Alpha should set the price at [£50] in order to achieve the target profit margin.

Task 3.12

To: Finance director **Subject:** Variances
From: Accounting technician **Date:** Today

(a) Sales volume

The sales volume is expected to double.

The volume increase will increase the profit margin if the fixed costs remain constant.

In this case the fixed production costs are remaining unchanged and therefore the increased volume will improve the gross profit margin (GPM).

Materials cost

The material cost per unit reduces by 20% to £4 per unit which will also improve the margin for the proposed position. The doubling of the volume is likely to allow the company to purchase in greater quantities and access additional discounts.

Labour cost

The labour cost per unit is unchanged and therefore has no effect on the margin.

There have been no economies of scale or learning effect.

Fixed production costs

The fixed production costs are constant in total but the important point is that they are spread over more units. The proposed position increases the volume by 2x (200%) which reduces the fixed cost per unit. Fixed costs per unit reduce by 50%. This will improve the margin for the proposed position.

(b) Inventory levels

Inventory levels are likely to increase significantly because the volume of demand is expected to be higher and therefore higher inventory levels will be needed to fulfil orders. Based upon the current inventory levels in relation to turnover the forecast position will be that inventory levels may increase to around £560,000 (current inventory days = 350,000/2,250,000 × 365 = 56.78 days, therefore inventory will become (£3.6 million/365) × 56.78 days = £560,000).

Trade receivable levels

Trade receivables' levels are likely to increase significantly because the turnover increases. The current position is that trade receivable days are 55.3 days (500/3,300) × 365. Therefore assuming similar profile trade receivables will increase to around £820k (5,400,000/365) × 55.3 = £818k.

Task 3.13

(a) Credit controller

Currently the assessment of creditworthiness, setting of credit limits, and chasing of debts is performed by sales staff. Sales staff may not have experience in credit control and may, while acting entirely with good intentions, extend credit to a customer who is not credit worthy. They could be tempted to give credit to customers without thoroughly checking their financial situation. Sales staff should not be responsible for chasing overdue receivables, as they may be reluctant to push hard for payment for fear of damaging the relationship with customers. They are also likely to see the task as low priority and prefer to spend their time generating sales and thereby gaining commission.

The new credit controller should perform a thorough assessment of new customers before setting a credit limit, which should be authorised by the sales manager. The credit controller should chase payment of overdue receivables, which should happen before they are 120 days overdue.

Sales manager

Sales staff have freedom to set sales discounts, and may set unrealistic discounts to achieve their sales targets. SSSL then loses out on potential revenue. Sales staff are also able to access the customer master file to enter discounts, which could result in fraud or error.

The sales manager should set out clear policies for the award of discounts and then authorise any discounts given. The sales manager should then update the master files. The sales manager should also introduce procedures to improve the documentation in the sales system, such as having sequentially numbered sales orders rather than an email to the accounting and despatch departments. As stated above, the sales manager should also authorise credit limits.

(b) Cost implications

SSSL will have additional payroll costs to bear. The credit controller's salary will be a fixed cost but the sales manager's salary is likely to be semi-variable, as the role is likely to carry some sales-related remuneration. These costs will increase the break-even point and impact on profit, although hopefully the involvement of the sales manager will increase sales and that of the credit controller will reduce bad debt expenses.

Resentment of sales staff

The filling of these two roles could cause resentment among sales staff. They will lose a lot of their freedom to operate autonomously, may interpret the appointments as being criticism of their abilities, and could be obstructive. They could leave SSSL, leaving the company with a shortage of experienced staff.

Task 3.14

If Roe were to stop being produced, the company would lose the benefit of the contribution generated by Roe, but would save on the fixed costs:

	£
Loss of contribution	(30,000)
Savings in fixed costs	10,000
Incremental loss	(20,000)

If production stopped on Roe, the company would see a fall of £20,000 in their profits.

The profit generated by Codlings would be as follows:

	£
Contribution	24,000
Directly attributable fixed costs	(12,000)
Incremental profit	12,000

If production was switched to Codlings, Gritby would only make £12,000 profit, so the company would suffer an overall drop in profits of £8,000.

They should, therefore, keep making Roe in preference to Codlings.

Task 3.15

(a)

	Blossom £000	
Revenue (2,850 × 1.4)	3,990.0	
Materials (784 × 1.4 × 0.95)	1,042.7	
Direct labour (448 × 1.4)	627.2	
Fixed production overheads (420 + 100)	520.0	
Cost of sales	2,189.9	
Gross profit	1,800.1	45.1%
Sales and distribution costs (640 × 1.4)	896.0	
Administration costs (250 + 60)	310.0	
Profit from operations	594.1	14.9%

(b) Dandelion should be closed down if the decision was based solely on the financial data.

(1) This is because the company will be more profitable:
(2) Current profit = £150,000 + £308,000 = £458,000
(3) New profit = £594,100

(c) **Any one of the following suggested answers.**

- **Staff morale** – staff will either need to be redeployed or made redundant, which negatively impacts morale and motivation.
- **Customers** – as the product made and sold by Dandelion is different from that of Blossom and the local retailers do not buy from both subsidiaries, it is possible that Daisy could adversely impact the success of these local retailers. The Dandelion range sources from local materials, which is its unique selling point. By ceasing this range, Daisy could adversely impact their company image, and potentially even impact the Blossom range's appeal.
- **Suppliers** – some suppliers may be reliant on the organisation to stay in business. If the organisation chooses to stop making the product this could have severe consequences on these local suppliers, especially the local wood supplier.

Task 3.16

(a) The loss of a proportion of financial and customer staff will probably have affected staff morale amongst the remaining staff in these departments. This could have affected their commitment to the company and been detrimental to the customer experience. Fewer staff could also have affected accuracy and there could potentially be errors in the accounts.

- The reduction in staff is likely to explain some of the reduction of £774,000 in administrative expenses (financial staff) and increase in distribution costs (of £1,010,000) due to the increase in warehouse staff.
- By moving the focus of the business to increasing sales, these sales may be made at all costs, with large discounts (affecting the gross profit) and/or risking higher bad debt levels. Controls need to be in place to ensure that sales staff are following company policies regarding discounting and offering credit.

- Flexing the budget will give a more useful figure for costs and revenues to compare with the actual costs and revenues generated. These variances will help to identify where sales are being made at the expense of profits caused by heavy discounting by sales staff.
- The company's profit has decreased, yet the corporation tax charge has risen. This may suggest issues regarding the computation of the tax during the year. There may be a lack of knowledge remaining in the financial department to complete the tax return correctly, and to take advantage of any reliefs.

(b)

- The company has increased its revenues by 12% and its gross profit by 16% which in a competitive market is very good. However, increased operating expenses have resulted in a reduction in operating profits of 20%.
- The gross margin is very high; this is not abnormal in this sector, especially for software (although the margin is high for hardware), but it may also be the result of errors, due to the staff turnover.
- Total expenses as a percentage of revenue have increased substantially in 20X3 (47%) compared with expenses in 20X2 (30%). The result of this has seen operating profit as a percentage of revenue reducing significantly year on year from 48% (20X2) to 34% (20X3).
- The increase in the distribution costs as a percentage of revenue (an increase of 5%) may reflect inefficiencies in the method of distribution in an industry that separates these functions.
- The administrative expenses as a percentage of revenue have halved from 13% to 7%, although they do not represent a significant amount in absolute terms. This is possibly due to the reduction in financial and administrative staff during the year.
- The increase in the selling expenses as a percentage of revenue by 18% may be as a result of the need for the company to spend more on advertising and the hiring of new sales staff.
- The reduction in profit before tax and the increased tax charge have resulted in a reduction in profit after tax of 43%.
- Total dividends have increased, despite the lower profits. This may be due to pressure from shareholders or a lack of investment in the business (by reinvesting profits made) as a Board of Directors decision.

Task 3.17

Overhead	Cost driver units (Working 1)	Cost driver rate	Overhead absorbed for X84 (Working 2)	Overhead absorbed for Y78 (Working 3)
£488,000	61,000 machine hours	£8 per machine hour	£288,000	£200,000
£85,000	50 production set-ups	£1,700 per production set-up	£17,000	£68,000
£162,000	36 orders	£4,500 per order	£72,000	£90,000
		Total overhead by product	*£377,000*	*£358,000*
		Quantity made	12,000	25,000
		Overhead absorbed per unit by product	**£31.42**	**£14.32**

Working 1

(3 × 12,000) + (1 × 25,000) = 61,000 machine hours

10 + 40 = 50 production set-ups

16 + 20 = 36 orders

Working 2

£8 × 3 × 12,000 = £288,000

£1,700 × 10 = £17,000

£4,500 × 16 = £72,000

Working 3

£8 × 1 × 25,000 = £200,000

£1,700 × 40 = £68,000

£4,500 × 20 = £90,000

Task 3.18

Cost pool	Overhead	Activity level	Overhead rate
Order processing	25% × £1,000,000 = £250,000	50,000 orders	£250,000 / 50,000 = £5 per order
Sales force salaries	40% × £1,000,000 = £400,000	20,000 hours	£400,000 / 20,000 = £20 per hour
Research and development	35% × £1,000,000 = £350,000	10,000 hours	£350,000 / 10,000 = £35 per hour

Total contribution = (£13,000,000 – £2,600,000 – £1,300,000) = £9,100,000

Contribution per unit = £9,100,000 / 130,000 units = £70 per unit

	£
Contribution from Customer X66 purchases = (1,000 units × £70 per unit)	70,000
Overheads attributable to Customer X66 = (400 order × £5 per order) + (300 hours × £20 per hour) + (100 hours × £35 per hour)	11,500
Profit attributable to Customer X66	**58,500**

Task 3.19

No

If product line K51 were to be shut down, the resulting incremental costs and revenues would be as follows:

	K51 £'000
Sales lost	(600)
Cost of production saved:	
Materials	200
Labour	95
Variable overhead	75
Fixed overhead (20% x £200)	40
Selling costs	40
Profit forgone	**150**

Conclusion

The shutdown of product line K51 would lead to a loss of profit of £150,000 and should therefore not go ahead.

Note. The amount of £150,000 profit forgone could also have been reached by considering the fixed costs that would still be incurred (80% of £200,000 = £160,000) minus the loss avoided from shutting down product line K51 (£10,000).

Task 3.20

Comparing the benefits lost and gained from replacing Product M4 with the newly developed product:

£	Product M4	New product
Contribution	(6,000) foregone	12,000 gained
Fixed costs	2,500 saved	(8,000) incurred
Profit/(loss)	(3,500) profit foregone	4,000 profit gained

Conclusion

While there is a financial benefit to be had from replacing Product M4 with the newly developed product (£4,000 – £3,500 = a net gain of £500) the current uncertainty over costs and the relatively small net gain mean that this decision is likely to require further information before an accurate conclusion can be reached.

Task 3.21

(a)

	Tracker £	Tracker plus £
Direct cost	60.00	80.00
Production overhead	3.00	4.50
Total cost	63.00	84.50

Workings

1 Direct cost Tracker: Materials (£40) + Labour (2 hours × £10) = £60

Direct cost Tracker plus: Materials (£50) + Labour (3 hours × £10) = £80

2 Production overhead:

OAR = Budgeted fixed overhead/budgeted activity

Budgeted fixed overhead = £100,000 + £140,000 = £240,000

Budgeted activity = (50,000 units × 2 hours) + (20,000 × 3 hours) = 160,000 hours

OAR = £240,000/160,000 = £1.50 per labour hour

Per Tracker: £1.50 × 2 hours = £3.00

Per Tracker plus: £1.50 × 3 hours = £4.50

(b)

	Tracker £	Tracker plus £
Direct costs	60.00	80.00
Inspection	1.45	1.38
IT support	0.70	5.25
Total cost	62.15	86.63

Workings

1 Inspection OAR: £100,000/(290 + 110) = £250 per inspection

Tracker total inspection cost = £250 × 290 = £72,500

Per unit = £72,500/50,000 = £1.45

Tracker plus total inspection cost = £250 × 110 = £27,500

Per unit = £27,500/20,000 = £1.375

2 IT support OAR: £140,000/(5,000 + 15,000) = £7 per support hour

Tracker total IT support cost = £7 × 5,000 hours = £35,000

Per unit = £35,000/50,000 = £0.70

Tracker plus total IT support cost = £7 × 15,000 = £105,000

Per unit = £105,000/20,000 = £5.25

(c) Under traditional absorption costing the Tracker plus watch has a higher production cost. This occurs for two reasons, firstly 50% more overhead cost attributed to it because it takes 50% more labour hours to manufacture each unit.

Secondly, the direct production costs are higher because of the higher direct material and direct labour costs.

When production was labour intensive this method is the most appropriate because it assumes that when more time is spent producing a product a greater share of the production overheads should be charged to a product.

However, the increase in technology in the production line would lead to a decrease in labour and the overheads will relate to machine hours rather than labour hours.

Under ABC there is a greater difference in the production cost of the two products, which can be attributed to the fact that the Tracker plus has three times as many IT support hours, perhaps because it is more complicated to manufacture as it is the plus product.

(d) ABC can provide a more accurate cost per unit.

ABC can provide insight into how activities drive costs and so recognises that costs are not just related to production and sales volume.

As technology increases, overhead often become a greater proportion of total costs and ABC can help managers understand how costs can be controlled.

(e) The use of technologies can help a business speed up many processes.

If technology is used to replace tasks which were time consuming this allows managers to focus on key areas.

Effective technology can therefore improve overall inefficiencies in the business. Specifically, for Digital Ltd, ABC can be aided by the improved technologies which have been implemented which will enable the information required to calculate cost drivers to be obtained more effectively.

Task 3.22

No

In order to make a decision about the future of the Advice division we need to consider the relevant costs and revenues. If the division was closed the following would be lost/saved:

	Advice **£**
Sales revenue	50,000
Variable labour cost	(20,000)
Contribution	30,000
Fixed operating costs*	(10,000)
Profit/(Loss)	20,000

*only 25% of the fixed operating costs are relevant as the remaining 75% are incurred regardless of whether the division is closed down. Therefore, Service Ltd would loose out on £20,000 of profit if it closed the division and overall company profit would fall to £25,000.

Chapter 4 – Ratio analysis

Task 4.1

	✓
Receivables days + Inventory days – Payables days	✓
Receivables days + Payables days – Inventory days	
Inventory days + Receivables days + Payables days	
Inventory days – Receivables days – Payables days	

Task 4.2

(a)

	✓
Understandability	
Relevance	✓
Comparability	
Faithful representation	✓

(b) Income is defined as:

'Increases in economic benefits during the accounting period in the form of inflows or enhancements of assets or decreases of liabilities that result in increases in equity, other than those relating to contributions from equity participants'.

Task 4.3

(a)

Return on equity	Profit after tax/Total equity × 100
Acid test ratio	(Current assets – Inventories)/Current liabilities
Inventory holding period	Inventories/Cost of sales × 365
Asset turnover (net assets)	Revenue/(Total assets – Current liabilities)
Gearing	Non-current liabilities/(Total equity + Non-current liabilities) × 100

(b) Ratios:

Ratio	Calculation	Working
Return on equity	**18.1%**	5,136/28,326
Acid test ratio	**0.9:1**	(13,192 – 6,724)/7,258
Inventory holding period	**58.3 days**	6,724/42,126 × 365
Asset turnover (net assets)	**1.2 times**	58,914/(55,984 – 7,258)
Gearing	**41.9%**	20,400/(28,326 + 20,400)

Task 4.4

(a) Current ratio

- Current ratio is better than the industry average
- Poole Ltd has more current assets available to meet its current liabilities/is more solvent
- However, the ratio looks to be too high and indicates less efficient management of working capital
- It may have higher levels of receivables, inventories or cash and cash equivalents/lower payables

Inventory turnover

- Inventory turnover is better than the industry average
- Poole Ltd is selling its inventories slightly more quickly as compared to the industry average
- Could be due to more effective inventory management systems or the company might have reduced its selling prices or employed better marketing techniques
- Leads to lower storage costs and there is less risk of stock obsolescence

Trade receivables collection period

- Trade receivables collection period is worse than the industry average
- Poole Ltd is taking longer to collect debts
- This is bad for cash flow
- Could be due to poor credit control procedures
- May just be offering longer credit terms to boost sales
- Could indicate the presence of irrecoverable debts

Trade payables payment period

- Trade payables payment period may be considered to be better than the industry average (if linked to supplier goodwill) or worse (if linked to cash flow)
- Poole Ltd is paying its trade suppliers sooner
- This is bad for cash flow
- This is good for supplier goodwill
- It may have negotiated additional settlement discounts with suppliers
- Suppliers may have dictated shorter payment terms

(b) Collect debts more quickly/reduce trade receivable days, eg improve debt collection procedures, reduce credit periods

Problem: possible loss of customers

Increase the length of time taken to pay suppliers/increase trade payable days, eg negotiate extended credit terms, improve payment procedures

Problem: may lose supplier goodwill/settlement discounts

Increase the inventory turnover by reducing the inventory holding

Problem: run the risk of a stock-out, which in turn, may reduce customer goodwill

Task 4.5

(a)

	✓
Financial perspectives of the company, such as profit margins	✓
Supplier perspectives, such as the number of supplier complaints	
Customer perspectives of the company, such as number of repeat orders	✓

The four perspectives of the Balanced Scorecard are: customer, financial, innovation and learning, and internal perspectives.

(b)

Abbas Ltd Balanced Scorecard	Year ended 31 Dec 20X4	Year ended 31 Dec 20X5	Working
Profitability and gearing:			
Gross profit %	54.3%	50.5%	8,640/17,120 × 100
Operating profit %	12.5%	12.6%	2,150/17,120 × 100
Return on capital employed	23.9%	26.0%	2,150/(7,190 + 1,070) × 100
Gearing	30.1%	13.0%	1070/(7190 + 1070) × 100
Liquidity ratios:			
Current ratio	2.9:1	2.6:1	(10,310 – 5,060)/(1,670 + 380)
Acid test/quick ratio	1.3:1	1.1:1	(2,010 + 340)/(1,670 + 380)
Working capital days:			
Inventory holding period	119 days	125 days	2,900/8,480 × 365
Trade receivables collection period	41 days	43 days	2,010/17,120 × 365
Trade payables payment period	55 days	72 days	1,670/8,480 × 365
Working capital cycle	105 days	96 days	125 + 43 – 72

(c) (i) Profitability

	✓
This has been a year of steady, if unspectacular, progress. Although profitability has dipped, the return on capital employed has been kept under control.	
The profitability ratios give cause for concern. The small increase in sales revenue has not improved the gross profit percentage. Operating expenses have increased, reducing operating profit and return on capital employed.	
The ratios give mixed messages. Some have improved and some have deteriorated. Further investigation is required.	✓

(ii) Gearing

	✓
The decreased gearing ratio is due to the repayment of non-current liabilities.	✓
It is likely that the interest cover ratio has decreased.	
The increased gearing ratio shows that the company has become more risky.	

(iii) Liquidity

	✓
Both ratios have deteriorated which indicates that the company is less solvent than last year; however, both ratios still fall within an acceptable level.	✓
Both ratios remain quite high, which may indicate that working capital is not being used effectively.	
Some liquidity ratios have improved and some have deteriorated. Further investigation is required to understand whether liquidity is improving.	

(iv) Working capital

	✓
The working capital cycle has worsened. The inventory holding period has improved but the other ratios indicate a lack of financial control.	
There is a welcome improvement in the working capital cycle, mainly due to the change in the payment period for payables.	✓
The working capital cycle is worse than a year ago because of the increased revenue.	

(v) Overall performance

	✓
Profitability has declined in 20X5. However, the gearing and liquidity measures show an improving financial position.	
20X5 has been a bad year. Profitability has declined and finances are coming under pressure.	
Steady progress has been made in 20X5. The ratios show that the company is being better managed.	✓

Task 4.6

Increase in the current ratio

This may indicate increased inventory, cash or receivable levels. The implications of this may be that the company is expanding, or alternatively that it is experiencing trading difficulties and is unable to sell its inventory or to collect its receivables. An increase may also be due to a decrease in trade payables or other current liabilities.

Decrease in gross profit margin

This may indicate that the cost of raw materials or bought-in goods has increased, or that discounts or selling prices have decreased. This may not be a bad thing if the reason for this is an overall increase in turnover.

Increase in inventory holding period

An increase in inventory holding period may indicate that the company is unable to sell its inventory. An increase can also indicate that the company is expecting additional sales, or simply that the business is expanding. Many businesses are cyclical and increases and decreases are to be expected.

An increase in gearing

Gearing is the relationship between equity and borrowings. A high level of gearing generally indicates that the company has a high level of borrowings and must pay fixed interest on the borrowings. This means that there is less available for shareholders but it may also mean that the company is expanding, which means greater returns for shareholders in the future. A high gearing ratio may mean that the company is at risk of financial problems.

Task 4.7

(a)

	✓
An architectural practice	
A supermarket	
An estate agent	
A manufacturer	✓

The high inventory turnover rules out the estate agency and architectural practice. Supermarkets can also have a high inventory turnover, but tend to operate on low profit margin.

(b)

	✓
5.1%	✓
4.7%	
6.6%	
6%	

	£000
Profit before interest and tax	230 %
Capital employed (3,500 + 1,000)	4,500
	= 5.1%

(c)

	✓
Reducing the receivables collection period	
Reducing the inventory holding period	
Reducing the payables payment period	✓
Reducing time taken to produce goods	

This will reduce working capital and means that it will take longer to build up working capital needed for production. The other options will all speed up the operating cycle.

(d)

	✓
3.9%	✓
7.6%	
16.1%	
7.1%	

Operating profit margin is a component of ROCE, so 16.3%/4.19 = 3.9%

Task 4.8

(a)

	Peas	Carrots
ROCE	$= \frac{(1,500 - 240) \times 100}{(5,500 + 3,000)}$ = 14.8%	$= \frac{(2,500 - 500) \times 100}{(2,800 + 6,200)}$ = 22.2%
Gross profit margin	= 1,500/12,000 × 100 = 12.5%	= 2,500/20,500 × 100 = 12.2%
Operating profit margin	$= \frac{(1,500 - 240) \times 100}{12,000}$ = 10.5%	$= \frac{(2,500 - 500) \times 100}{20,500}$ = 9.8%
Current ratio	= 5,000/4,100 = 1.2:1	= 7,300/5,700 = 1.3:1
Closing inventory holding period	$= \frac{2,000}{10,500} \times 365$ = 70 days	$= \frac{3,600}{18,000} \times 365$ = 73 days
Trade receivables collection period	$= \frac{2,400}{12,000} \times 365$ = 73 days	$= \frac{3,700}{20,500} \times 365$ = 66 days
Trade payables payment period	$= \frac{3,100}{10,500} \times 365$ = 108 days	$= \frac{3,800}{18,000} \times 365$ = 77 days
Gearing	$= \frac{3,000 \times 100}{(3,000 + 5,500)}$ = 35.3%	$= \frac{6,200 \times 100}{(6,200 + 2,800)}$ = 68.9%
Interest cover	$= \frac{(1,050 + 210)}{210}$ = 6 times	$= \frac{(1,400 + 600)}{600}$ = 3.3 times
Dividend cover	= 900/250 = 3.6 times	= 1,000/700 = 1.4 times

(b) **Profitability**

Carrots has an ROCE 50% higher than Peas, which is driven by the higher sales and operating profits values. Carrots's operating profit is 60% higher than Peas's operating profit. They both have a similar capital employed. This means that Carrots is more efficient at using its resources to generate income.

The gross profit margins and operating profit margins are very similar, meaning that they are equally good at controlling their costs.

Gearing

Carrots has approximately double the gearing of Peas, due to its higher borrowings. Carrots's interest cover is 3.3 times compared to six times for Peas, making its level of risk higher.

In a bad year Carrots could have trouble servicing its debts and have nothing left to pay to shareholders.

However, the fact that Carrots has chosen to operate with a higher level of gearing rather than raise funds from a share issue also increases the potential return to shareholders.

Liquidity

Peas and Carrots have broadly similar current ratios, but showing a slightly higher level of risk in the case of Carrots. Carrots is also running an overdraft while Peas has a positive cash balance.

Peas is pursuing its receivables slightly less aggressively than Carrots, but taking significantly longer to pay its suppliers.

As this does not appear to be due to shortage of cash, it must be due to Peas being able to negotiate more favourable terms than Carrots.

Summary

Carrots has a higher revenue than Peas and a policy of paying out most of its earnings to shareholders. This makes it an attractive proposition from a shareholder viewpoint.

However, if its revenue were to fall, there would be little left to distribute. This is the risk and return of a highly geared company.

Carrots is already running an overdraft and so has no cash to invest in any more plant and equipment. In light of this, its dividend policy is not particularly wise. Peas has a lower revenue and a much more conservative dividend policy but may be a better long-term investment.

Forrest's decision will probably depend upon its attitude to risk and the relative purchase prices of Peas and Carrots.

Task 4.9

(a)

	20X1	20X0
Net profit %	= 3,000/25,500 × 100 = 11.8%	= 2,500/17,250 × 100 = 14.5%
Operating profit %	= 5,900/25,500 × 100 = 23.1%	= 3,600/17,250 × 100 = 20.9%
Gross profit %	= 10,700/25,500 × 100 = 42%	= 6,900/17,250 × 100 = 40%
ROCE	= 5,900/18,500 × 100 = 31.9%	= 3,600/9,250 × 100 = 38.9%
ROE	= 3,000/9,500 = 31.6%	= 2,500/7,250 = 34.5%

	20X1	20X0
Gearing	= 9,000/(9,000 + 9,500) × 100 = 48.7%	= 2,000/(2,000 + 7,250) × 100 = 21.6%
Interest cover	= 5,900/650 = 9.1 times	= 3,600/100 = 36 times
Current ratio	= 6,000/5,200 = 1.2:1	= 7,200/3,350 = 2.2: 1
Quick ratio	= (6,000 – 3,600)/5,200 = 0.5:1	= (7,200 – 1,800)/3,350 = 1.6:1

(b) Profitability

Revenue has increased by 48% while profit for the year has only increased by 20%. However, on closer inspection, we can see that this is to a large degree attributable to the tax charge for the year. The pre-tax profit has increased by 50%, which is in line with the increased revenue.

We do not have a breakdown of the tax charge but it could include underpayments in previous years, which distorts the trading results.

The gross profit margin and operating profit margin are very similar to the prior year, both showing a slight improvement.

There has been a significant increase in capital employed during the year ended 31.12. 20X1. There is an additional £12.3 million in non-current assets, financed from a new issue of 8% loan notes. This has had the effect of reducing the return on capital employed slightly, but not nearly as much as would be expected, indicating that the investment is already producing returns.

The return on equity is skewed by the tax charge, without which, it would be showing a slight increase due to the increased profits.

Gearing

The increase in loan capital does have significance for shareholders. The interest charge has increased from £100,000 to £650,000, which reduces the amount available for dividends.

Gearing has increased significantly. The rate that TTP has to offer to loan note holders has already increased from 5% to 8%. If it required further borrowing, with this high gearing, it would have to pay substantially more.

Shares in TTP have become a riskier investment. One indicator of this is the interest cover, which has fallen from 36 times to 9 times.

Liquidity

The area in which there is most cause for concern is liquidity. Cash has fallen by £4.2 million and the company is now running an overdraft.

It has tax to pay of £2.2 million and this will incur penalties if it is not paid on time. The current ratio has declined from 2.1:1 to 1.2:1 and the quick ratio, which indicates the immediate cash situation, shows a fall from 1.6:1 to 0.5:1, which is a dangerous position to be in.

Summary

Overall, shareholders should be reassured that TTP is profitable and expanding. The company has perhaps overstretched itself and significantly raised its gearing, but it is to be hoped that the investment for which this cash was presumably used will bring in future returns, which should help with the liquidity issues, as long as the company manages to stay solvent until then.

Chapter 5 – Internal controls

Task 5.1

Rees Ltd's plan is [an incremental] change.

The fact that the time of Rees Ltd's accounting staff will be freed up by not having to complete cheques by hand is [a tangible benefit of the change] .

Task 5.2

(a) A key strength is that no customer order for even a single high-value item is accepted without authorisation by the sales manager, and higher value orders must also be approved by the sales director. This reduces the exposure of the company to incurring the cost of making bespoke furniture to customer order and then finding that it is not actually a valid sale.

(b) There does not appear to be a firm price agreed with the customer for the furniture ordered. It may be that the uncertainty surrounds discounts or the firm price is agreed once production have priced each job. If this is the case then the procedures need to be explicit on this point. If in fact there is no firm price agreed then the business is exposed to the risk that the customer, on receipt of the goods, refuses to pay or only pays a smaller sum than the company is due.

(c) As well as a firm price being agreed with the customer at the time the order is taken, and this being approved by the sales manager and sales director where relevant, the company should get the customer to pay a deposit to the company. This will give it more assurance that the furniture will be accepted and fully paid for once delivered. It will also improve the company's working capital cycle.

Task 5.3

(a) The procedures include a robust process for ensuring that orders are taken only from new customers who represent a good credit risk. It is also a strength that, depending on the outcome of the checks, the sales manager has the discretion to require payment in full upfront or payment on credit terms. The business benefits from these in that there should be no irrecoverable debts, and cash flow should be maintained.

(b) It is possibly a weakness that credit checks etc are only performed on new customers. Existing customers should also be reviewed, depending on their history with the company and the length of time since they last bought. As it is the company may still be exposed to poor payment.

It is a serious weakness that the accounts receivable clerk creates and posts invoices, has sole discretion to issue credit notes, and identifies and posts receipts. This lack of segregation of duties creates a serious risk of fraud by the clerk, alone or in collusion with a customer. The sales manager should authorise invoices and credit notes, and someone else should be responsible for identifying receipts and posting them.

(c) It seems strange that a credit customer is offered 15% discount for early payment, when no such discount is offered to customers who must pay in advance. It is possible that orders are being lost through this policy, or alternatively that revenue for an agreed sale is being lost unnecessarily. The company could consider offering a discount to cash customers, and a reduced discount to early-paying credit customers.

Task 5.4

(a) **(i)** The highest value items – for production and for capital expenditure – require senior management authority before being ordered, and all purchases except the most minor require proper purchase orders. Staff understand therefore that proper procedures must be followed before items can be purchased, which reduces the risk of unnecessary items being bought by the company or that staff will purchase items for themselves at the company's expense.

(ii) A coherent approach is taken towards negotiating credit terms with suppliers, which benefits the company's cash flow and planning.

(b) **(i)** It appears items can be purchased from suppliers without a price having been agreed upon. This introduces unnecessary uncertainty into the company's costs and cash flows, and may mean that some items that should be authorised are bought without authority. The remedy is that no purchase orders may be raised without an agreed price being stated on them.

(ii) There is no security over the purchase order forms, so in theory any staff member or other person may obtain a form and purchase items to the account of Sleeptight Ltd. This means the company may be liable to pay for items it has not received or does not want. Purchases should not be allowed to proceed unless a purchase order number, taken from the purchase order book which is kept securely, is notified to the supplier.

(iii) Outside of production materials and capital expenditure there is no need for higher authority and no cash limit on an individual purchase. In theory this could result in an entire budget being spent inappropriately. All purchases above a certain amount should be authorised by the finance director.

(c) Negotiations by the purchasing manager with suppliers seem to focus only on how long the company can take to pay. There is an opportunity to expand the role of the purchasing manager to (1) guide and authorise budget holders in their purchases and (2) negotiate prices, delivery terms and discounts with existing and new suppliers.

Task 5.5

(a) There appears to be good co-ordination between ordering and receiving goods, with Goods Inwards expecting receipts since they have the copy orders. They also check the goods before agreeing they are acceptable by signing the documentation and forwarding to accounts so the subsequent invoice can be recorded. These strengths help to ensure that only goods ordered are received, recorded and paid for, and those goods are of acceptable quality. This will help the company's profits.

(b) There is a serious lack of segregation of duties in the accounting function as the same person (the accounts payable clerk) records invoices, asks for credit notes, decides on payment and makes payment. This increases the risk that through collusion or alone, the clerk could engage in fraud, or could make mistakes that are not corrected (especially overpaying, which is unlikely to be complained about by suppliers). At least one other person should be involved in processing, recording, authorising and paying invoices. A third person should be responsible for reviewing figures and procedures.

Task 5.6

(a) The company maintains a good system of recording and validating production hours spent on individual items of furniture via the job sheets completed by production workers and checked by supervisors. This means the company has a good idea of how much in terms of labour it costs to produce each item, so the company can ensure it covers its costs for each item.

(b) **(i)** There is no check over signing in and out by production workers. As the payroll clerk prepares wages on the basis of the signing-in book, this means that the company may be paying for hours not worked. In addition the signing-in book should be kept in a secure place and should be checked and authorised by managers/supervisors.

(ii) There is no segregation of duties with regard to payroll accounting, so the payroll clerk may be making mistakes/committing fraud without any checks. In particular the accounts manager should be responsible for authorising amendments to standing data, especially for leavers and joiners, for reviewing the reconciliation of the wages control account, and for authorising or processing bank transfers.

(c) The hours recorded in the signing-in book could be reconciled to the hours of productive work recorded on the job sheets. This would help as a sense check on both records and would also help to identify idle time.

Task 5.7

Transaction stream	Risk	Control objective	Control activity
Purchasing	Company pays for goods it does not receive	Ensure all payments are only made for goods actually received, and which are in accordance with the order	Examine goods in for quality and quantity and reconcile the goods to the original order. Issue a goods received note, which is matched to the invoice prior to payment.
Sales	Sales recorded late so fines incurred from HMRC with respect to VAT	Record invoices in the correct time period	Implement cut-off procedures.
Payroll	Company overpays	Pay employees the correct, authorised gross pay	Refer to standing data when calculating wages and salaries. Implement good timekeeping controls, which are used in the wages calculation.

Task 5.8

(a) The original budgeted profit was £73,300 based on budgeted sales of 178,000 units. The actual profit of £80,100 was achieved by selling 192,000 units, some 8% higher sales volume than budgeted.

The original budgeted sales price was £7.20 per unit, while the actual sales price achieved was slightly less at £7.17 per unit.

The main factor leading to the increase in profit was therefore the significant increase in sales volume which more than compensated for the fall in price achieved.

Some categories of costs, eg labour and administration, reported favourable variances in the operating report, which additionally contributed to the increase in profit.

(b) It is possible that there may have been errors in the prices charged to customers. Internal controls over the use of price lists when invoicing, and the completeness of sales recording, should be checked.

Similarly, there may have been errors in processing and recording purchases underlying the costs, or there may have been poor purchasing procedures so that the best deal on prices was not secured.

Task 5.9

Transaction stream	Risk	Control objective	Control activity
Payroll	Company incurs fines from HMRC	Ensure all deductions have been properly calculated and authorised	Reconcile total pay and deductions in wages control account regularly. Ensure up-to-date tax codes are used for each employee.
Sales	Custom lost through chasing payments already made by the customer	Bank and record all money received accurately	Reconcile the bank account regularly and ensure all receipts are allocated to the correct sales ledger account.
Purchasing	Company pays the wrong supplier	Record invoices in the correct purchases ledger account	Reconcile supplier statements with the purchases ledger accounts.

Task 5.10

(a) Tangible costs are easily identified, quantifiable costs of the change for example buying a new software package. These costs can be calculated based on evidence such as invoices or timesheets. Tangible costs associated with training might include:

- Cost of training course
- Cost of lost chargeable hours (as the staff will not be working on clients' accounts)
- Travel expenses to the training provider

Intangible costs are costs of the change that are more difficult to identify and quantify eg the cost of lost custom as customers go elsewhere during the disruption caused by the change. These might include:

- Other staff feeling discontent as new staff are provided with training which they did not have
- Loss of efficiency as new staff's induction is extended and therefore they are not available for client work
- Client dissatisfaction at delays in completion of work due to staff not being available

(b) Costs of the system

- Cost of staff time – preparing the data for migration to the new system and assisting the software contractors.
- The cost of the 'learning curve' whereby staff will be slower initially on the new software whilst they practise using it. There may initially be teething problems eg being able to use the reports and understanding what the system can and cannot do.
- Cost of implementing the new system:
  - Full system initial cost £10,800
  - Annual ongoing cost £3,300
- Having an integrated system would lead to reduced calculation errors, simpler and faster online reporting (to HM Revenue and Customs for PAYE) and closer monitoring of the inventory chain.
- Initial training costs will be dependent on how many staff will be trained. If at least 10 staff members (including both directors) are trained, it would be cost-effective to have an in-house training programme. The financial outlay would be the same as sending all 10 to college, but it would reduce the travel expenses.
- The downside would be that 10 people would be unavailable to perform business work on the day of training.
- Crachett & Co may consider sending selected members of staff to college to complete the learning; for example five staff members costing £275 each, total cost of £1,375, and these staff could act as 'champions' and assist those members of staff who will complete the online training (such as more restricted users, maybe more junior members of the team or administration or support staff).
- The training programme selected will need to be considered in terms of the financial costs, plus the opportunity costs of staff being unavailable to undertake client work.
- Timing of the change onto the new software would need to be considered as there is a need to think about any downtime from the system; the training time especially in the busy seasons around Christmas and March year ends.
- Staff discontent amongst those not chosen to receive training on the new system. Additionally some staff may get different levels of training, such as some going to college for the course and others completing the online course. This may lower staff morale and productivity.
- Staff completing the online course; there is a risk that they will not complete the training in line with the launch of the new system. The licence allows six months access, so staff using the online training will need to be reviewed to ensure they have completed it on time.

Workings

Training costs

£2,700 for 15 people is £180 per person

For the same outlay, albeit training people at college, this is £275 per person. Therefore it is cost-effective if 10 people at least are trained at the in-house course (£2,700/275 = 9.8).

Benefits of the system

- Staff are better trained in basic knowledge and skills so they are more efficient.
- Staff morale improves as they feel valued due to the investment in training them, increasing their motivation.
- Customers see well-trained and knowledgeable staff so the company's reputation is enhanced, leading to more repeat custom and recommendations from satisfied customers.
- If everyone is trained at the same time (such as using the in-house training), staff can discuss issues with each other rather than struggling on alone. It will act as a team-building exercise and improve morale.
- More efficient working practices, as the bookkeeping, financial reporting and tax reporting will be integrated in the new system, leading to fewer errors and missing information. This could improve profit margins as staff will take less time to complete the client work.

Conclusion

The partners of Crachett & Co should consider the long term as well as the short term implications of the new software. The new software will enable the firm to become more efficient and also ensure all updates to the software are completed in a timely manner. Although the costs are initially high (financially and in terms of staff time and effort), the longer-term efficiencies and the ability to grow the business will enable Crachett & Co to benefit in the long term.

AAT EPAL4 PRACTICE ASSESSMENT 1
LEVEL 4 SYNOPTIC ASSESSMENT

Time allowed: 3 hours

PRACTICE ASSESSMENT 1

Level 4 Synoptic Assessment AAT practice assessment 1

Company background and history

SL Products Ltd (SLP) is a market-leading manufacturing business supplying advanced technological electronics to a number of companies around the world.

The company operates through a manufacturing division and a sales division. The manufacturing division supplies electronics to the sales division, which sells both its own manufactured product and other complementary products that it buys in from third parties.

SLP has its head office on an industrial estate in Manchester, where its management team and accounts department are both based. Its main manufacturing plant is also on this site, as is the sales division's offices and large central warehouse.

SLP was established 10 years ago by three of its four founding shareholders, Shaun Murphy, Colin Smith and Cynthia Moss. Six years ago they sold most of their shareholding in the business, and now do not have a controlling interest.

Louise Harding was brought into the company and joined the board as Finance Director just over 18 months ago when the other directors and main shareholders realised the company's urgent need to have more high-level professional accounting expertise.

Over the past 10 years, the company has grown rapidly and in the year ended 31 December 20X1 it had a turnover of £20 million. It also now employs around 400 full-time equivalent employees. However, profits from operations have fallen in recent years.

In an attempt to improve profitability, SLP has recently acquired a controlling interest in Merville Ltd, a small manufacturing business that offers unique, patented products that are complementary to those manufactured by SLP. Merville Ltd has prepared initial accounts for its first year of trading under the control of SLP.

A management bonus is linked to these results but it has not yet been authorised for payment by SLP's remuneration committee.

SLP's mission statement

We aim to be a market-focused business that specialises in the research, manufacture and distribution of passive electronic components.

Our priority is providing a great service and a product range at the cutting-edge of technology. We offer our customers cost-effective products of the highest quality.

We aim to develop long-term relationships with all our stakeholders and deal with suppliers, customers and our staff with the highest levels of integrity.

Developments in the market

During the past few years, the company has been feeling the effects of a recession. Intense competition from overseas manufacturers, made worse by the strength of the pound, has led to a progressive lowering of market prices within the areas in which SLP operates.

It is also becoming increasingly difficult for small companies like SLP to compete with the Research and Development (R&D) budgets available to larger businesses. As the pace of technological change in electronics has accelerated, the company's product range has gradually lost the lead it once had in cutting-edge technology.

The directors have now reluctantly decided that they may be forced to downsize some parts of the business that they spent the past 10 years building up. On the other hand, as they are unable to outspend their bigger competitors on R&D, they are looking to acquire stakes in companies like Merville Ltd to fill the resulting gaps in their product range.

SLP's strategic planning and control

When Louise Harding joined SLP, she suggested that they need to view it from different perspectives rather than just focus on its financial results. The directors and the controlling shareholders agreed to develop measures, collect data and judge the company's performance relative to each of these perspectives. These measures have now been in place for a full year and have just been reviewed.

Perspective 1

The first perspective involves employee training and having corporate cultural attitudes that relate to both individual and corporate self-improvement. In an organisation, such as SLP, that relies on problem solving and creative thinking, its people are an important resource. In a market characterised by rapid technological change, it is necessary for staff to be in a continuous learning mode.

Measures were put into place to focus training and development funds where they could help the most.

This perspective, which recognises that 'learning' is more than 'training', also considers aspects such as the effectiveness of mentoring within the organisation, as well as the ease of communication among workers that allows them to get help with a problem easily, when needed.

In general, the first year's results show that the company has performed well in relation to this perspective.

Perspective 2

The second perspective refers to internal business processes. Measures based on this perspective allow the directors to see how well their business is running, and whether its products and services conform to customer requirements (as per its mission statement).

Those who know these processes most intimately, namely the various line managers within SLP, carefully designed these measures.

In general, the first year's results show that the company has performed poorly in relation to this perspective. This is because the business is gradually losing its technological lead in several of its products.

Perspective 3

The third perspective relates to how SLP's customers view the business. Cynthia Moss has stressed the importance of customer focus and customer satisfaction. She has emphasised that these are leading indicators; if customers are not satisfied, they will eventually find other suppliers that will meet their needs better. Poor performance on this perspective is therefore a key indicator of future decline, even though the current financial results may still look reasonable.

To develop measures for customer satisfaction, SLP examined its customers both in terms of the kinds of customers they are, and the kinds of products that they are buying from SLP.

The first year's results indicate that customers were generally satisfied with the customer care and service, but were less satisfied with some of the older products in the product range that were overdue for replacement.

Interestingly, customers were generally more satisfied with the bought-in products being sold by the sales division than those manufactured in-house by SLP itself. There was considerable interest in the new products manufactured by Merville Ltd.

Perspective 4

The fourth and final perspective is the traditional outlook using financial data. Louise Harding instigated the use of more accurate and timely monthly management accounts immediately after she was appointed. She argued that the previous focus on only financial data had led to an 'unbalanced' situation with no attention having been paid to the real drivers of business performance.

The financial results continue to show falling profits which the other three perspectives help to explain.

Strategy-mapping

SLP has used the first year's results to carry out a strategy-mapping exercise (strategy maps are communication tools used to tell a story of how value is created for the organisation. They show a logical, step-by-step connection between strategic objectives in the form of causes and effects).

Generally speaking, improving performance in the objectives from the first of SLP's perspectives will enable it to improve its internal processes. This will enable it to improve its results for customer satisfaction and eventually its financial performance.

This implies that SLP needs to reallocate resources towards increasing its R&D spend which will, in turn, redirect its internal processes towards new product development. This should result in improved customer satisfaction and retention, with the final outcome being increased profitability.

Some of the directors, however, believe that the root cause of SLP's problems lies in exactly the matters that are under the Finance Director's direct control, ie the problems are due to poor internal controls and systemic weaknesses. The directors also point out that they will struggle to finance any increase in R&D.

At this point in time, the board is divided and uncertain how best to proceed.

Staff

SLP's key personnel are as follows:

Managing director	Shaun Murphy
Finance director	Louise Harding
Production director	Colin Smith
Sales director	Cynthia Moss
Chief accountant	Sue Hughes
Purchasing manager	Tony Clark
Warehouse manager	Robert Utley
Credit controller	Ray Massey
Accounts payable clerk	Liz Hall
Accounts receivable clerk	Matthew Tunnock
General accounts clerk and cashier	Hina Khan
Payroll clerk	Jane Patel

SLP's financial statements

The financial statements for SLP for the year ended 31 December 20X1 show that the company had a turnover of £20 million, and made a profit after tax of £960,000.

These accounts do not include the results of Merville Ltd, which was acquired on 1 January 20X2.

SL Products Ltd – Group statement of profit or loss for the year ended 31 December 20X1

Continuing operations	£000
Revenue	20,000
Cost of sales	(14,322)
Gross profit	5,678
Operating expenses	(4,413)
Profit from operations	1,265
Finance costs	(47)
Profit before tax	1,218
Tax	(258)
Profit for the period from continuing operations	960

SL Products Ltd – Group statement of financial position as at 31 December 20X1

	£000
ASSETS	
Non-current assets	
Property, plant and equipment	4,330
	4,330
Current assets	
Inventories	3,614
Trade receivables	2,976
Cash and cash equivalents	8
	6,598
Total assets	10,928
EQUITY AND LIABILITIES	
Equity	
Ordinary share capital (£1 shares)	800
Share premium	1,160
Retained earnings	4,065
Total equity	6,025
Non-current liabilities	
Bank loans	1,200
	1,200

£000
Current liabilities	
Trade payables	3,360
Bank overdraft	124
Tax liabilities	219
	3,703
Total liabilities	4,903
Total equity and liabilities	10,928

Task 1 (20 marks)

Louise Harding, the Finance Director of SL Products Ltd has asked you to analyse the published results of a competitor business. Until recently, you were employed by that business. Therefore, you have a detailed understanding of its financial position.

(a) Answer the following questions.

Which of your principles is threatened by this request?

Confidentiality ▼

Picklist:

Confidentiality
Objectivity
Professional competence and due care

How should you respond?

Base on publisheld ▼
results

Picklist:

Base your analysis entirely on the published results ✓
Obtain the competitor's agreement ✗
Refuse to do the analysis ✗

(4 marks)

Hina Khan, the Cashier of SL Products Ltd, is preparing a cash flow forecast. She asks which of the following are cash flow items.

(b) Show whether each of the following should be included in a cash flow forecast by selecting your answers from the picklist.

Revaluation of premises

Do not ▼

Bonus issue of shares in SL Products Ltd

Included ▼

Payment of dividend on ordinary shares

Included ▼

Write off obsolete inventory

[do not ▼] ✓

Picklist:

Do not include in cash flow
Include in cash flow

(8 marks)

Liz Hall, the Accounts Payable Clerk, asks for you for advice. She wants to know whether the following errors and discrepancies would be detected by reconciling the accounts payable ledger to its control account.

(c) Show whether each of the following errors and discrepancies would be detected by reconciling the accounts payable ledger to its control account by selecting your answers from the picklist.

Errors and discrepancies	Answer
A supplier has been paid for an invoice twice	▼ Would ✗
A supplier invoice has been posted to the wrong supplier account	▼ Would not ✓
A cheque payment has been debited to the accounts receivable control account	▼ Would ✓
VAT on some purchases has been omitted from the VAT return	▼ Would not ✓
A purchase invoice has been debited to the account of a supplier	▼ Would ✓

Picklist:

Would be detected
Would not be detected

(5 marks)

Liz Hall maintains the accounts payable ledger. Her duties include ensuring the accounts payable ledger agrees to its control account.

(d) What sort of access should Liz have to the accounts payable control account?

[Read only ▼]

Picklist:

Full access, including data entry
No access
Read only access

(1 mark)

An inventory count is to take place at SL Products Ltd's financial year end. Sue Hughes, Chief Accountant, is concerned that the inventory value will appear to be too high. She suggests that all inventory receipts in the final week of December should be dated 1 January and that those items should be excluded from the count. The relevant purchase invoices would be posted in the new accounting period.

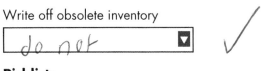

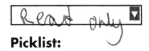

(e) Which of the following statements describes this suggestion?

	✓
Acceptable commercial practice	
Unethical 'window dressing'	✓
Fraud	
Breach of the control environment	

(2 marks)

Task 2 (20 marks)

This task contains parts (a) and (b).

You have been asked to review the adequacy of the controls in SL Products Ltd's payroll and purchasing procedures.

(a) Identify whether each of the following control activities would help ensure that correct payroll payments are made to employees. (5 marks)

Activity	Would help	Would not help
Payroll liabilities to HMRC are paid when due.		✓
Payroll is authorised by the Payroll Manager before processing.	✓	
Payslips are posted direct to employees' home addresses.		✓
Overtime claims are approved by departmental managers.	✓	
Accounting for payroll is performed by the general ledger team.		✓

Your review of the purchasing procedures has established the following information.

The company operates an integrated accounting system which includes a purchase accounting module. Tony Clark, the Purchasing Manager, is responsible for managing purchasing activities.

Ordering and receipt:

- All purchases, except petty cash items, must be documented on an official purchase order. The order should state the agreed price, if known.
- All departments are provided with books of pre-numbered order forms. These books can be obtained from the stationery store.
- Orders for production materials and items for resale must be signed by Robert Utley, the warehouse manager.
- Capital expenditure orders must be signed by Louise Harding, the finance director.
- There is no cash limit for purchase orders provided that they are within the approved budget.
- Other orders must be signed by the relevant budget holders.

- Four copies of the order form are printed. Once signed, the original is sent to the supplier. A copy printed on yellow paper is sent to Liz Hall, the accounts payable clerk. Two further copies, printed on pink and green paper, are retained by the individual who raised the order.
- When the goods or service(s) are received, the individual who raised the order signs the green copy and sends it to Liz Hall. This individual retains the pink copy for their files.

New suppliers:

- New suppliers are contacted by Tony Clark. He provides a trade reference and banking details and requests credit terms.
- He usually requests payment terms as either of the following:
  - Two months from the end of the month in which delivery takes place
  - A 5% discount for payment within 21 days of delivery

  However, terms are subject to negotiation.
- Tony enters the agreed supplier details and payment terms into the supplier master file.

Accounting:

- All purchase invoices are checked by Liz Hall. She checks the calculations, matches the invoices to appropriate yellow and green copy orders and clears the invoices for payment.
- Liz posts the cleared invoices to the computerised accounting system.
- Liz takes up queries with suppliers, requesting credit notes when appropriate.
- Invoices are automatically paid as they fall due through the bankers automated clearing system (BACS). Liz authorises one payment run every week.

Complete your review as follows, using the provided answer spaces below:

(b) (i) Identify FIVE systemic weaknesses in the company's internal controls for handling purchases on credit. (5 marks)

(ii) Explain how each weakness that you have identified could create a problem for the company. (10 marks)

Note. You are **not** required to make recommendations to change procedures.

No.	Weakness	Potential problem

No.	Weakness	Potential problem

Task 3 (20 marks)

This task contains parts (a) to (d).

(a) Match the appropriate stage of the product life cycle to each description.

(5 marks)

Description	Stage
Steep upward trend in revenue.	growth ▼
New products enter market and demand starts to fall.	Decline ▼
High costs incurred but no revenue generated.	Development ▼
Economies of scale achieved, and advertising costs are low.	maturity ▼
High advertising costs but low revenue levels.	Introduction ▼

Picklist:

~~Decline~~
~~Development~~
Growth
~~Introduction~~
Maturity

Review of product pricing

The latest annual results of SL Products Ltd have confirmed the trend of decline in the gross profit margin. The Board of Directors has asked Cynthia Moss (Sales Director) and Louise Harding (Finance Director) to review the situation and report back with an agreed proposal.

The company operates in a very competitive, high-tech market. It is necessary to create a stream of innovative new products that are as good as, or better than, those marketed by competitors. Meanwhile, older products rapidly go into decline. It is almost impossible to increase the price of a product after it is launched.

Louise proposes that all new products should be priced to give a 30% mark-up over cost. She says, 'We only get one chance to get the price right. Production costs are always rising but we cannot increase our prices. If we launch the products with a 30% mark-up, they will be profitable for a few years.'

Sue Hughes, the chief accountant, has created a simple spreadsheet model to determine the selling prices for new products. She has used this model to calculate the selling price of two new products that are ready for launch.

Pricing spreadsheet

Sue explains that this is a full overhead recovery pricing model.

The variable element of production overheads is equal to 15% of the direct costs. (The direct costs are all variable.) Marketing and administration costs are fixed.

Prices for new products	£ per unit	
	NP1	NP2
Direct cost	18.00	42.00
Production overhead	3.60	8.40
Marketing and administration	5.40	12.60
30% mark-up	8.10	18.90
Selling price	35.10	81.90

Sales Director's response:

Cynthia says that the spreadsheet prices are not competitive.

She knows that the business will suffer if she cannot refresh the product range with new products at attractive prices.

She has compared each of the two products (NP1 and NP2) with competitors' products and has estimated the sales potential at three price levels.

Price levels and estimated annual volumes	NP1		NP2	
	£ each	Volume	£ each	Volume
To undercut competition	21.00	250	52.00	600
Market price	28.00	150	60.00	400
Spreadsheet price	35.10	50	81.90	150

Cynthia asks you to calculate which prices would be most profitable.

(b) For each product calculate the marginal cost per unit and the annual contribution that would be earned at each of the two prices that Cynthia has considered.

Calculation of contribution	NP1 £	NP2 £
Marginal cost per unit (to the nearest penny)		

Annual contribution	£	£
To undercut the competition		
Market price		
Spreadsheet price		

(8 marks)

(c) Select the price that would give the highest contribution to profit for each of the two products.

Product	Best price
NP1	▼
NP2	▼

Picklist:

Market price
Spreadsheet price
To undercut the competition

(2 marks)

(d) Discuss the possible impact of Louise Harding's proposed policy on the business.

(5 marks)

Task 4 (20 marks)

This task contains parts (a) and (b).

Louise Harding, the Finance Director, is preparing a presentation for the Board of Directors. She has asked you to complete a comparative 'score card' of key financial ratios which she will use as part of her presentation.

Relevant data has been extracted from the last two years' accounts. These extracts do not include the results of Merville Ltd.

Extracts from accounts of SL Products Ltd	Year ended 31 December 20X1 £000	Year ended 31 December 20X2 £000
Sales revenue	20,000	20,900
Cost of sales	14,322	15,144
Profit from operations	1,265	470
Assets		
Non-current assets	4,330	4,234
Inventories	3,614	3,908
Trade receivables	2,976	3,032
Cash and equivalents	8	6
Total	**10,928**	**11,180**
Equity and Liabilities		
Equity	6,025	5,550
Non-current liabilities	1,200	1,400
Trade payables	3,360	3,730
Bank overdraft	124	260
Tax liabilities	219	240
Total	**10,928**	**11,180**

(a) Complete the scorecard by calculating the missing ratios.

SL Products Ltd Scorecard	Year ended 31 Dec 20X1	Year ended 31 Dec 20X2
Profitability and gearing (correct to 1 dp):		
Gross profit %	28.4%	%
Operating profit %	6.3%	2.2%
Return on capital employed	17.5%	%
Gearing	16.6%	20.1%

SL Products Ltd Scorecard	Year ended 31 Dec 20X1	Year ended 31 Dec 20X2
Liquidity ratios (correct to 1 dp):		
Current ratio	1.8:1	:1
Acid test/quick ratio	0.8:1	:1
Working capital days (correct to nearest day):		
Inventory holding period	92 days	94 days
Trade receivables collection period	54 days	53 days
Trade payables payment period	86 days	90 days
Working capital cycle	60 days	days

(10 marks)

(b) Select the ONE correct observation about each aspect of business performance below.

Profitability

	✓
This has been a year of steady, if unspectacular, progress. Although profitability has dipped, the return on capital employed has been kept under control.	
The profitability ratios give cause for concern. The small increase in sales revenue has not improved the gross profit percentage. Operating expenses have increased, reducing operating profit and return on capital employed.	
Some have improved and some have deteriorated. Further investigation is required to understand whether profitability is improving.	

(2 marks)

Gearing

	✓
The increased gearing ratio is entirely due to the increase in non-current liabilities.	
It is likely that the interest cover ratio has increased.	
The increased gearing ratio shows that the company has become more risky.	

(2 marks)

Liquidity

	✓
Both ratios have deteriorated which indicates that the company is less solvent.	
Both ratios remain too high, indicating that working capital is not being used effectively.	
The ratios are contradictory. Further investigation is required.	

(2 marks)

Working capital

	✓
The working capital cycle has worsened. The inventory holding period has improved but the other ratios indicate a lack of financial control.	
There is a welcome improvement in the working capital cycle, mainly due to the change in the payment period for payables.	
The working capital cycle is worse than a year ago because of the increased cost of sales.	

(2 marks)

Overall performance

	✓
Profitability has declined in 20X2, mainly due to competitive pressures. However, the gearing and liquidity measures show an improving financial position.	
20X2 has been a bad year. Profitability has declined and finances are coming under pressure.	
Steady progress has been made in 20X2. The ratios show that the company is being better managed.	

(2 marks)

Task 5 (20 marks)

This task contains parts (a) to (d).

(a) Identify whether each of the following statements in relation to organisational structure is true or false. (5 marks)

Statement	True	False
The chain of command relates to the number of staff that the manager is directly responsible for.		
Tall organisations typically only have a few layers of management.		
The span of control represents the number of layers of management in the organisation.		
Flat organisations will have a shorter scalar chain than tall organisations.		
Decentralised organisations typically allow lower levels of management greater authority than centralised organisations.		

Louise Harding, the finance director, has been contacted by Colin Smith, the production director, due to several complaints by his team with respect to errors in their monthly pay.

Louise was somewhat surprised to hear of these problems as only two months ago a new payroll system was introduced. The new system was intended to reduce the current level of errors and improve the overall efficiency of the payroll function. Louise has undertaken a review.

The only member of staff in the payroll department is Jane Patel, the payroll clerk. Jane reports directly to Sue Hughes, the chief accountant.

Jane has been with SL Products Ltd for nine years and is very experienced. The payroll team used to have another payroll clerk, Hazel Copeland, who started with the company at the same time as Jane, but she resigned from the company nine months ago. Sue Hughes decided that there was no need to replace Hazel as a new updated payroll system would be introduced.

Both Jane and Hazel had been struggling to cope with the payroll workload due to the rapid expansion of SL Products Ltd but the situation deteriorated further with the acquisition of Merville Ltd and the increased demands that it placed in terms of payroll processing.

It took over six months from Hazel resigning for the new payroll system to be introduced as Sue was very busy managing the accounting issues arising from the acquisition of Merville Ltd. During this time Jane was very unsupported and working long hours, and errors started to creep into the pay of employees.

The new payroll system allows Colin to authorise and input production bonuses payable to his production team. All that is then required is for Jane to use an automatic feature within the payroll system to allocate these bonus payments to the relevant staff member. The bonus payments have been problematic with many staff members complaining to Jane about errors or of not being paid their bonus at all. Where staff have been overpaid, Colin has decided that it would be too stressful to ask staff to repay the month and didn't want the senior management team to know. He told Jane to charge the overpayments to his departmental budget.

Training for the new payroll system was supposed to have taken place in the first week of operation. The training was scheduled for Jane and Sue however Jane was the only one to attend, and, due to work pressures, Jane had to cut short the training so that she could meet the payroll deadline.

Many of the features within the new system are not being used due to the lack of training. With the acquisition of Merville Ltd there have been further complications as the staff have different contractual entitlements from those at SL Products Ltd, particularly in relation to employee benefits. The HR department at Merville Ltd has been helpful, but also quite slow, and therefore issues have arisen before the correct information has been received by Jane.

At Merville Ltd the administration of the overall benefit scheme had been outsourced to a third party and that continues to be the case with a fee of £2,500 a month payable to the third party.

(b) Prepare a SWOT analysis of the payroll department of SL Products Ltd, identifying TWO factors for each element.

Strengths

(2 marks)

Weaknesses

(2 marks)

Opportunities

(2 marks)

Threats

(2 marks)

(c) (i) Recommend TWO improvements to the current payroll system.

(2 marks)

(ii) Identify TWO benefits that EACH improvement would bring to the payroll system. **(4 marks)**

First recommended improvement	Benefits to the payroll system

Second recommended improvement	Benefits to the payroll system

(d) Identify ONE ethical issue currently facing SL Products Ltd.

(1 mark)

AAT EPAL4 PRACTICE ASSESSMENT 1
LEVEL 4 SYNOPTIC ASSESSMENT

ANSWERS

Level 4 Synoptic Assessment
AAT practice assessment 1

Task 1 (20 marks)

(a) Which of your principles is threatened by this request?

Confidentiality

How should you respond?

Base your analysis entirely on the published results

(4 marks)

(b) Revaluation of premises

Do not include in cash flow

Bonus issue of shares in SL Products Ltd

Do not include in cash flow

Payment of dividend on ordinary shares

Include in cash flow

Write off obsolete inventory

Do not include in cash flow

(8 marks)

(c) Show whether each of the following errors and discrepancies would be detected by reconciling the accounts payable ledger to its control account by selecting your answers from the picklist.

Errors and discrepancies	Answer
A supplier has been paid for an invoice twice	Would not be detected
A supplier invoice has been posted to the wrong supplier account	Would not be detected
A cheque payment has been debited to the accounts receivable control account	Would be detected
VAT on some purchases has been omitted from the VAT return	Would not be detected
A purchase invoice has been debited to the account of a supplier	Would be detected

(d) What sort of access should Liz have to the accounts payable control account?

Read only access

Liz only needs to view the data, so she does not need to change any data and therefore does not need 'full access, including data entry'. However, she needs read access so that she can ensure the accounts payable ledger agrees to its control account. Therefore, 'read only access' is appropriate for her role.

(1 mark)

(e) Which of the following describes this suggestion?

	✓
Acceptable commercial practice	
Unethical 'window dressing'	✓
Fraud	
Breach of the control environment	

(2 marks)

Task 2 (20 marks)

(a) Identify whether each of the following control activities would help ensure that correct payroll payments are made to employees. (5 marks)

Activity	Would help	Would not help
Payroll liabilities to HMRC are paid when due.		X
Payroll is authorised by the Payroll Manager before processing.	X	
Payslips are posted direct to employees' home addresses.		X
Overtime claims are approved by departmental managers.	X	
Accounting for payroll is performed by the general ledger team.		X

Complete your review as follows, using the provided answer spaces below:

(b) (i) Identify five systemic weaknesses in the company's internal controls for handling purchases on credit.

(ii) Explain how each weakness that you have identified could create a problem for the company.

Note. There are more suggested answers shown below than are required to be given in the task. Awarded 1 mark for identification of the weakness and 2 for the explanation (with a maximum of 3 for each point).

No.	Weakness	Potential problem
1	The purchasing manager appears to have very little involvement in day-to-day purchasing, apart from negotiating terms with new suppliers.	Failures in the system and system abuses could go unnoticed.
2	No apparent security for order stationery.	Potential for anyone to commit fraud by making purchases for their own use in the company's name.

No.	Weakness	Potential problem
3	Budget holders and the warehouse manager can raise orders and sign that the goods or services have been received.	There is a potential for fraud as there does not appear to be any check that these purchases are necessary, or even for business use.
4	The procedures do not include any mention of checking that goods and services of the correct standard have been received.	If this is not happening the company could be paying for unsatisfactory supplies.
5	There is no cash limit to purchase orders provided that they are within the approved budget.	Without a second signature on large purchases, there is scope for errors, poor judgement or fraud to be very costly.
6	Orders can be placed without agreeing a price.	The company is in a weak position to negotiate price after the goods or service have been received.
7	Lack of authorisation of new accounts.	There should be a policy for choosing new suppliers. Potential for fraud through collusion with suppliers.
8	The terms agreed by Tony Clark are not countersigned.	Potential for fraud through collusion with suppliers.
9	Only one signature is required on purchase orders.	Potential for fraud through collusion with suppliers.
10	Liz Hall checks, clears and arranges payment of invoices.	Potential for fraud through collusion with suppliers.
11	Tony Clark and Liz Hall control all aspects of purchase accounting.	Potential for fraud through collusion.

(15 marks)

Task 3 (20 marks)

(a) Match the appropriate stage of the product life cycle to each description.
(5 marks)

Description	Stage
Steep upward trend in revenue.	Growth
New products enter market and demand starts to fall.	Decline
High costs incurred but no revenue generated.	Development
Economies of scale achieved, and advertising costs are low.	Maturity
High advertising costs but low revenue levels.	Introduction

(b) For each product calculate the marginal cost per unit and the annual contribution that would be earned at each of the two prices that Cynthia has considered.

Calculation of contribution	NP1 £	NP2 £
Marginal cost per unit (to the nearest penny)	20.70	48.30

Working: direct cost + (15% × direct cost)

Annual contribution	£	£
To undercut the competition	75	2,220
Market price	1,095	4,680
Spreadsheet price	720	5,040

(8 marks)

(c) Select the price that would give the highest contribution to profit for each of the two products

Product	Best price
NP1	Market price
NP2	Spreadsheet price

(2 marks)

(d) Indicative content:

- Proposed policy would ensure that all new products are profitable:
  - Any price that is higher than marginal cost will contribute and therefore increase profits
  - The policy generates prices which are greater than total unit cost, including an apportionment of fixed costs
  - Therefore, all products should be profitable at any volume of sales
- Despite being profitable, the new policy could be damaging to the business:
  - The pricing policy does not allow the sales director to respond to market conditions and find the combination of profit and volume that will optimise contribution
  - SLP is in a price competitive business
  - If new products are not priced competitively they will only sell in small volumes
  - As ageing products decline they must be replaced by innovative new ones.
  - The business will go into decline if the product range is not refreshed.

0 marks: No response worthy of credit

1 – 2 marks: Limited range of impacts discussed, with some reference made to the proposed policy that would ensure all new products are profitable. Limited reference made to the new policy being damaging to the business.

3 – 4 marks: Range of impacts discussed with some use of evidence to support all products being profitable; some reference made to potential impacts to the business due to the competitive environment.

5 marks: To achieve full marks, the response will be well balanced including a wide range of factors which demonstrates clear understanding that the proposed policy, despite being profitable, would be damaging to the business. Good use of evidence to support discussion.

(5 marks)

Task 4 (20 marks)

(a) Complete the scorecard by calculating the missing ratios.

SL Products Ltd Scorecard	Year ended 31 Dec 20X1	Year ended 31 Dec 20X2
Profitability and gearing (correct to 1 dp):		
Gross profit %	28.4%	**27.5** %
Operating profit %	6.3%	2.2%
Return on capital employed	17.5%	**6.8** %
Gearing	16.6%	20.1%
Liquidity ratios (correct to 1 dp):		
Current ratio	1.8:1	**1.6** :1
Acid test/quick ratio	0.8:1	**0.7** :1
Working capital days (correct to nearest day):		
Inventory holding period	92 days	94 days
Trade receivables collection period	54 days	53 days
Trade payables payment period	86 days	90 days
Working capital cycle	60 days	**57** days

(10 marks)

(b) Select the ONE correct observation about each aspect of business performance below.

Profitability

	✓
This has been a year of steady, if unspectacular, progress. Although profitability has dipped, the return on capital employed has been kept under control.	
The profitability ratios give cause for concern. The small increase in sales revenue has not improved the gross profit percentage. Operating expenses have increased, reducing operating profit and return on capital employed.	✓
Some have improved and some have deteriorated. Further investigation is required to understand whether profitability is improving.	

(2 marks)

Gearing

	✓
The increased gearing ratio is entirely due to the increase in non-current liabilities.	
It is likely that the interest cover ratio has increased.	
The increased gearing ratio shows that the company has become more risky.	✓

(2 marks)

Liquidity

	✓
Both ratios have deteriorated which indicates that the company is less solvent.	✓
Both ratios remain too high, indicating that working capital is not being used effectively.	
The ratios are contradictory. Further investigation is required.	

(2 marks)

Working capital

	✓
The working capital cycle has worsened. The inventory holding period has improved but the other ratios indicate a lack of financial control.	
There is a welcome improvement in the working capital cycle, mainly due to the change in the payment period for payables.	✓
The working capital cycle is worse than a year ago because of the increased cost of sales.	

(2 marks)

Overall performance

	✓
Profitability has declined in 20X2, mainly due to competitive pressures. However, the gearing and liquidity measures show an improving financial position.	
20X2 has been a bad year. Profitability has declined and finances are coming under pressure.	✓
Steady progress has been made in 20X2. The ratios show that the company is being better managed.	

(2 marks)

Task 5 (20 marks)

(a) Identify whether each of the following statements in relation to organisational structure is true or false. **(5 marks)**

Statement	True	False
The chain of command relates to the number of staff that the manager is directly responsible for.		X
Tall organisations typically only have a few layers of management.		X
The span of control represents the number of layers of management in the organisation.		X
Flat organisations will have a shorter scalar chain than tall organisations.	X	
Decentralised organisations typically allow lower levels of management greater authority than centralised organisations.	X	

(b) Prepare a SWOT analysis of the payroll department at SL Products Ltd, identifying TWO factors for each element.

Strengths (2 marks)

- New payroll system introduced
- Jane has been with SL Products Ltd for 9 years
- Jane is an experienced payroll clerk
- New system allows the Production Director to input and authorise team bonuses
- Merville Ltd HR department helpful
- Any other relevant point.

Weaknesses (2 marks)

- Errors in the calculation of staff pay
- Payroll team understaffed as Hazel not replaced
- Sue too busy to assist Jane
- Merville Ltd HR department slow to respond
- Jane has only had partial training
- Training of department heads has not taken place
- Many features of the new payroll system not being used
- Any other relevant point

Opportunities (2 marks)

- Recruit an additional team member to the payroll team
- Provide full training to Jane and other relevant managers
- Avoid £2,500 a month fee by bringing benefit scheme administration in-house
- Use features of new payroll system not currently utilised
- Consider whether it might be appropriate to outsource the payroll department
- Any other relevant point

Threats (2 marks)

- Jane leaving would put SLP at risk of not meeting its legal obligations to staff
- Financial statements being incorrect
- Over-payments to staff who may subsequently leave company
- Risk of incorrect returns to HMRC and resultant penalties
- Any other relevant point

(8 marks)

(c) (i) Recommend TWO improvements to the current payroll system
(2 marks)

(ii) Identify TWO benefits that EACH improvement would bring to the payroll system
(4 marks)

Recommendation (1 mark)	**Benefits** (1 mark per benefit, max 2 per recommendation)
Start using the full features of the new payroll system	- Increased efficiency - Improved management information
Recruit a new payroll clerk / manager	- Increased resources should help to reduce errors - Ease burden on Jane
Formal training programme to be complete	- Managers can take advantage of features within new system - More accurate payroll
Bring administration of Merville Ltd in-house	- Save monthly fee - Opportunity to look at margining employment terms of staff
Any other relevant issues	

(d) Identify ONE ethical issue currently facing SL Products Ltd.

Colin is charging overpayments to the company accounts to avoid senior management becoming aware of payroll problems.

(1 mark)

AAT EPAL4 PRACTICE ASSESSMENT 2
LEVEL 4 SYNOPTIC ASSESSMENT

You are advised to attempt this practice assessment online from the AAT website. This will ensure you are prepared for how the assessment will be presented on the AAT's system when you attempt the real assessment. Please access the assessment using the address below:

https://www.aat.org.uk/training/study-support/search

The AAT may call the assessments on their website, under study support resources, either a 'practice assessment' or 'sample assessment'.

AAT EPAL4
PRACTICE ASSESSMENT 2

Scenario Overview
LEVEL 4 SYNOPTIC ASSESSMENT

Argent Electric Motors Ltd

For live assessments from 30 January 2023

Your live assessment will be based on this Argent Electric Motors Ltd scenario. BPP Practice Assessment 3 is also based on this scenario.

The other BPP Practice Assessments are based on the AAT sample scenario, SL Products Ltd, which was included before AAT Practice Assessment 1 at page 113.

Scenario

Version correct as at 17 August 2023; please check online at www.aat.org.uk to ensure you have the latest version

ARGENT ELECTRIC MOTORS LTD

Company background and history

Argent Electric Motors Ltd (AEM Ltd) sells both new and used electric cars. AEM Ltd was established three years ago and is owned by the four directors who created the company, all of whom continue to work full-time within the business and form its senior management team.

All the directors previously worked for one of the largest motor vehicle retailers in the UK and have extensive knowledge of the motor vehicle industry. They established AEM Ltd to take advantage of the increased demand for electric motor vehicles arising from both increased consumer demand for more environmentally friendly vehicles and the introduction of UK government legislation phasing out the sale of new gasoline cars.

The company operates 15 car showrooms across the UK where customers can view the different models and take advantage of the opportunity to test drive a vehicle. In addition, AEM Ltd sells cars via their website. All used cars are sold with a two-year warranty and free breakdown cover with a national motoring organisation. Customers have the option to purchase a fixed cost three-year servicing plan at a guaranteed minimum 20% discount off the standard servicing price schedule. The company also provides a price match promise for any new car purchased online.

Over the past three years AEM Ltd has grown rapidly and now has a turnover of over £40 million and employs more than 250 full-time employees.

Company philosophy

The environmental benefits of electric vehicles are at the core of the AEM Ltd brand. The reduction in emissions from electric vehicles, lower carbon footprint and noise reduction are the focus for all marketing campaigns undertaken by AEM Ltd.

Operationally, AEM Ltd also looks to minimise its impact on the environment. All showrooms are designed to reduce energy consumption and the organisations within its supply chain are assessed for their approach to sustainability before AEM Ltd works with them.

The business also understands the competitive nature of the car retailing market in the UK and through its price promise looks to provide the highest levels of value for money to its customers.

Operating model

AEM LTd has its head office in an industrial estate in Wembley in northwest London. All the management team, finance and other central services are based at this location. The site also has a large warehouse, from which it distributes the vehicles sold online directly to customers.

Operational costs need to be kept as low as possible to allow AEM Ltd to price match against its competitors so effective inventory management is fundamental. Managers at the UK showrooms are given inventory turnover targets for used cars and a threshold is established for the total level of vehicle parts held at each location.

Market developments

The level of ownership of electric vehicles has dramatically increased over the three years that AEM Ltd has been operating and competition in the marketplace is increasing as a result. However, the AEM Ltd brand remains strong and is helping the business continue to grow.

To further expand the business AEM Ltd has recently acquired Weldon Vehicles Ltd (WV Ltd). Although not noted for selling electric vehicles, WV Ltd has four showrooms in the north of England and has an excellent reputation.

AEM Ltd Performance Appraisal

Over the first two years the performance of the business was primarily assessed based on its financial results. The senior management team concluded that as the business was more established, a rounded approach should be taken to assessing performance, and it was decided that a balanced scorecard, analysing a wider range of areas, should be adopted.

Perspective 1 – How customers view the business

The senior management team view customer perception of the business as a fundamental element of its future success. There are two distinct elements to this: customer experience and satisfaction when acquiring a vehicle, and then the ongoing relationship with respect to servicing and support over their ownership of the vehicle.

The data shows that customer satisfaction is high when purchasing a vehicle but that the ongoing aftercare performance is disappointing.

Perspective 2 – Employee development

AEM Ltd's focus is to provide a workplace where employees develop their abilities and skills through training, and to provide a culture which encourages learning and development to take place. The car-sale industry has a reputation for low levels of staff engagement and loyalty to their employer.

Formalised induction courses have been introduced and all new staff are assigned a mentor whose role is to offer guidance and support. An extensive internal training programme has been established and staff are encouraged to contribute to the staff suggestion scheme.

Overall performance in this area has been positive, although feedback suggests that while many good features have been introduced, the culture within the business is that they are not promoted or encouraged.

Perspective 3 – Internal efficiency

Developing and maintaining internal processes is seen as crucial to the business. Functions such as vehicle deliveries, after-sales service and supplier relationships need to be as efficient as possible to deliver the growth wanted by the senior management team.

Performance in this area has been strong.

Perspective 4 – Financial performance

Although there has been a good start to the business it is important that the financial fundamentals of the business remain strong.

Encouragingly, the business continues to achieve solid growth in its financial performance. However, with the recent acquisition of WV Ltd, there is some concern that the business might be developing too quickly for its capital base.

Staff

Some of AEM Ltd's key personnel are listed below:

Chief Executive	Andrew Watts
Finance Director	Alison Clockwell
Operations Director	William Glass
Sales & Marketing Director	Barbara Sinta
Financial Controller	Chris Davies
Purchasing Manager	Graham Musa
Warehouse Manager	Susan March
Credit Controller	Ellen Peterson
Accounts Payable Clerk	Vinod Albert
Accounts Receivable Clerk	Billy Stark
General Accounts Clerk and Cashier	Katrina Walter
Payroll Clerk	John Morris

Argent Electric Motors Ltd financial statements

(Note that these do not include the results of Weldon Vehicles Ltd, which was acquired in January 20X3.)

Argent Electric Motors Ltd

Statement of profit or loss for the year ended 31 December 20X2

Continuing operations	£000
Revenue	40,230
Cost of sales	(28,750)
Gross profit	11,480
Operating expenses	(9,100)
Profit from operations	2,380
Finance costs	(495)
Profit before tax	1,885
Tax	(360)
Profit for the period from continuing operations	1,525

Argent Electric Motors Ltd

Statement of financial position as at 31 December 20X2

	£000
ASSETS	
Non-current assets	
Property, plant and equipment	2,170
	2,170
Current assets	
Inventories	4,885
Trade receivables	950
Cash and cash equivalents	945
	6,780
Total assets	8,950
EQUITY AND LIABILITIES	
Equity	
Ordinary share capital (£1 shares)	400
Retained earnings	2,035
Total equity	2,435
Non-current liabilities	
Bank loan	3,200
Current liabilities	
Trade payables	2,955
Tax liabilities	360
	3,315
Total liabilities	6,515
Total equity and liabilities	8,950

Synoptic assessment
Analysis of scenario: Argent Electric Motors Ltd

For assessment starting January 2023, AAT have issued a new live pre-release scenario, Argent Electric Motors Ltd (www.aat.org.uk/training/study-support/search).

It is essential that you have reviewed this prior to sitting your assessment. The synoptic assessment is designed to test your knowledge and application skills, and pull them together to demonstrate strong problem-solving techniques.

Here is a summary of some of the key points from the pre-release information. This is not an exhaustive analysis, and there are areas which would benefit from further review and investigation.

You will be given narratives as well as financial information during the assessment in addition to the pre-release information. This is not available before the assessment, so be prepared to use this additional resource and adapt your answers accordingly.

If possible, investigate the financial statements of similar companies in the car sales sector. You can then see whether the ratios and metrics from Argent Electric Motors Ltd appear reasonable.

A word on ratios: Ratios should be commented on, not just calculated and stated. If the information is available, compare it with previous years or to competitors' results. Consider what the ratio is telling you. If you are asked to discuss or explain or conclude information from a ratio, ensure you have given a justification for the movement (provided it is sensible and supported by facts, you will gain credit).

Key information provided

Please note that this information is not exhaustive and will give you a start on your pre-assessment analysis of the scenario.

Overall analysis of the pre-release material

One way of analysing a company is to draw up a SWOT analysis.

You may be asked to use this information to provide a report to the Board of Directors discussing some of these elements.

Ensure that you are familiar with producing a variety of reports, including a balanced scorecard based on the SWOT analysis. You may also be asked to comment about some of the strengths, weaknesses, opportunities and threats identified.

The following is not exhaustive and you are encouraged to build on this SWOT analysis to become familiar with the scenario and potential areas of risk.

Strengths	Weaknesses
- Directors have extensive knowledge of the motor vehicle industry - Strong company growth - Company philosophy to minimise environmental impact - Recognised brand name - New acquisition has a strong reputation - High customer satisfaction when acquiring new vehicles - Good internal efficiency	- After sales customer satisfaction scores are poor - Employee development ideas are not always embedded in the culture of the business
Opportunities	**Threats**
- Increased demand for electric motor vehicles	- Changes to government policy around electric vehicles - Consumer demand for electric vehicles decreases - Increased competition in the online car market

Further steps

- Calculate ratios on the pre-release information as far as the information allows.
- Ensure you understand the benefits and issues with using certain ratios and can justify why you have used those particular ratios and not others.
- Review the financial statements of companies in the car sales sector, as this will broaden your knowledge and potentially highlight more issues which businesses in this sector can face, for example, Motorpoint Group plc.
- AAT like to bring current issues in their Level 4 *Professional Accounting Apprenticeship Synoptic* assessment, so it is advisable to read financial papers, online news or look up financial statements on Companies House website. Some of these useful links will give you some material to start with.
- Please note that this list is not exhaustive and there may be elements for further discussion you have spotted or you think are relevant to the scenario.

Useful links

Electric models drive second-hand care sales higher (2022). BBC News. Available at https://www.bbc.co.uk/news/business-61383855 [Accessed 1 May 2024].

Lookers plc electric sales race ahead but profits stall (2022). Proactive Investors. Available at https://www.proactiveinvestors.co.uk/companies/news/990860/lookers-electric-vehicle-sales-race-ahead-but-profits-stall-990860.html [Accessed 1 May 2024].

Why electric cars will take over sooner than you think (2021). BBC News. Available at https://www.bbc.co.uk/news/business-57253947 [Accessed 1 May 2024].

Dealers cannot sell electric vehicles they do not have (2022). Financial Times. Available at https://www.ft.com/content/74541b00-eca9-412f-9227-3ba460ebfa82 [Accessed 1 May 2024].

How workshops might adapt to electric vehicle repairs and servicing (2022). Automotive Management Online. Available at: https://www.am-online.com/dealer-management/aftersales/how-workshops-might-adapt-to-electric-vehicle-repairs-and-services [Accessed 1 May 2024].

Tenfold expansion in chargepoints by 2030 as government drives EV revolution. UK Government. Available at https://www.gov.uk/government/news/tenfold-expansion-in-chargepoints-by-2030-as-government-drives-ev-revolution [Accessed 1 May 2024].

BPP PRACTICE ASSESSMENT 1
LEVEL 4 SYNOPTIC ASSESSMENT

Time allowed: 3 hours

PRACTICE ASSESSMENT 1

Level 4 Synoptic Assessment
BPP practice assessment 1

This practice assessment is based on the same scenario as AAT's practice assessment, SL Products Ltd. See pages 113–117 for the relevant pre-reading material.

Task 1 (20 marks)

(a) Complete the following statement.

The statutory duty to report whether SL Products Ltd's financial statements show a true and fair view is that of [▼].

Picklist:

Companies House
Sue Hughes, the chief accountant
the company's directors
the company's auditors

(2 marks)

At SL Products Ltd, the duties of processing purchase invoices, purchases ledger and processing payments are separated from each other. Tony Clark, purchasing manager, discovers that a goods returned note has not been followed up by a supplier's accounts department. No credit note has been received or posted to the purchases ledger.

(b) What is the correct action for Tony Clark to take?

	✓
Prepare a journal to record the necessary reversal of the purchase invoice	
Prepare a debit note and send it to the supplier	
Advise the accounts payable clerk of the omission	
Advise Liz Hall, the accounts payable clerk, to reverse the relevant invoice from the purchases day book	

(2 marks)

(c) Matthew Tunnock, the accounts receivable clerk, has asked you to show whether the following errors would be detected by reconciling the sales ledger to the sales ledger control account.

VAT on a sales invoice posted to sales instead of VAT control	▼
A sales invoice credited to the customer's account	▼
A sales invoice posted to the wrong customer account	▼
A batch of purchase invoices posted to the sales ledger control account	▼
A pricing error in a sales invoice	▼

Picklist:

Would be detected
Would not be detected

(5 marks)

You have been asked to set up an 8-character password for SL Products Ltd's accounting system.

(d) Which of the following would be the most secure?

	✓
98765432	
acsystem	
1jan2000	
?win121#	

(2 marks)

Your duties at SL Products Ltd include running credit checks on new customers. Recently the company has offered a large credit limit to Howlsons Ltd. Its finance director has sent you the following email to thank you for your support:

'Thank you for helping us agree terms of trade with SL Products Ltd. Now that our two companies are connected in this way I trust you will share with me any information you have about BFA Ltd, who also buys from you and who is our biggest competitor.'

(e) Answer the following questions.

Which of your fundamental principles is threatened by this request?

	▼

Picklist:

Confidentiality
Objectivity
Professional behaviour

What action should you take?

	▼

Picklist:

You can share some information but must advise BFA Ltd
You must notify the National Crime Agency of the request
You must refuse to share any information

(4 marks)

Louise Harding, the Financial Director has asked you to look at the management accounts. She wants you to determine who will be performing the analysis and has asked you to classify the different types of information.

(f) Identify the type of information provided in the following management reports

Wastage reports from the production line	▼
Inventory turnover reports	▼
Inventory level reports	▼
Future demand estimates for the next 12 months	▼
Analysis of competitor's products and their market positioning	▼

Picklist:

Operational
Strategic
Tactical

(5 marks)

Task 2 (20 marks)

This task contains parts (a) and (b).

(a) Match the appropriate category of internal controls to each description

(5 marks)

Description	Category of internal control
Checking the VAT calculation on an invoice before processing	▼
Review of the daily unallocated cash report from the receivables ledger by the financial controller	▼
Preparation of the supplier payment run by the cashier, rather than the purchase ledger clerk	▼
Each employee has a written job description and a clear chain of management	▼
Two factor authentication is required to access the cloud accounting software	▼

Picklist:

Physical
Management
Segregation of duties
Arithmetic
Organisational

You have been asked to review the adequacy of the control in SL Products Ltd's sales procedures. Your review has established the following information.

The company operates an integrated accounting system which includes a sales accounting module. Cynthia Moss, the Sales Director, is responsible for managing sales activities.

Ordering and despatch:

- All sales, except those for cash, must be documented on an official customer order. The order should state the agreed price, if known.
- Customer orders must be reviewed and signed by Cynthia Moss.
- Large orders must be signed by Louise Harding, the Finance Director.
- Five copies of the customer order form are printed. Once signed, the original is sent to the customer as an acknowledgement. A copy printed on yellow paper is sent to Matthew Tunnock, the accounts receivable clerk. A pink copy is sent to production and a green copy is sent to despatch. The orange copy is retained by the individual who took the order.
- When the goods are completed, production signs the pink copy and sends it to despatch.
- When the goods are sent out, despatch signs the green copy and sends it, with the pink copy, to Matthew Tunnock.

New customers:

- New customers are contacted by Ray Massey, the Credit Controller. He asks for a trade reference and banking details, and offers credit terms.
- He usually offers payment terms as follows:
  - One month from the end of the month in which delivery takes place.
  - With a 5% discount for payment within 21 days of delivery.

  However, terms are subject to negotiation.

Accounting:

- All sales invoices are raised by Matthew Tunnock. He matches yellow, pink and green copy orders and prepares the invoices for sending to the customer.
- He posts the invoices to the computerised accounting system.
- He answers queries from customers, issuing credit notes when appropriate.
- Most customers pay by bank transfer. Matthew Tunnock checks the bank account weekly and posts receipts to the ledger accounts.

Complete your review as follows:

(b) (i) Identify FIVE systemic weaknesses in the company's internal controls for handling sales on credit.

(ii) Explain how each weakness that you have identified could create a problem for the company.

Note. You are **not** required to make recommendations to change procedures.

No.	Weakness	Potential problem
1		
2		
3		
4		
5		

(15 marks)

Task 3 (20 marks)

This task contains parts (a) to (e).

(a) Match the cost type to each description. **(5 marks)**

Description	Cost type
Purchases of non-current assets or the improvement of the earning capability of non-current assets	▼
Cost which is fixed for a short range and then increases in steps	▼
Costs that can be specifically attributed to a cost unit	▼
Costs that change directly in line with any change in activity level	▼
The total of all direct costs	▼

Picklist:

Direct cost
Prime cost
Semi-fixed cost
Variable cost
Capital expenditure

Review of product pricing

SL Products Ltd has recently suffered a further decline in its gross profit margin. Cynthia Moss (Sales Director) and Louise Harding (Finance Director) are reviewing the situation so they can report to the Board of Directors with proposals to halt the decline.

The market for the company's high-tech products is very competitive, and success depends on constant innovation and better quality than competitor products. After about two years, a product enters the decline phase of its product life-cycle, when there is no scope for price increases and the likelihood of obsolete inventory.

Sue Hughes, the Chief Accountant, proposes that all new products should be priced to give a 25% margin on sales price, to generate as much profit as possible in the early years. She tells you there are two new products that are ready for launch: the AB, the CD and the EF.

The company uses a full overhead recovery pricing model. Variable production overheads are equal to 20% of materials and labour, which are all variable.

(b) Complete the calculation of the proposed selling prices based on a 25% margin.

Prices for new products	£ per unit	
	AB	CD
Materials and labour	72.00	45.00
Variable production overheads		
Fixed production overheads	6.00	3.00
Other fixed overheads	6.30	3.60
Total cost		
Price at 25% margin		

(4 marks)

Cynthia Moss, the sales director, says that Sue's approach to pricing may not be competitive. She has compared each of the two products (AB and CD) with competitors' products and has estimated the sales potential at three price levels; one at the price you calculated in (a), one which is designed to be cheaper than competitor prices, and one at market price.

Price levels and estimated annual volumes	AB		CD	
	£ each	Volume	£ each	Volume
Price at 25% margin	See (a)	175	See (a)	250
Cheaper than competitor price	125.00	300	65.00	500
Market price	130.00	275	75.00	300

Cynthia wants you to calculate which prices would be most profitable.

(c) For each product, calculate the marginal cost per unit and the annual contribution that would be earned based on each price and volume.

	AB £	CD £
Marginal cost per unit		
Annual contribution if price level is...		
...price at 25% margin		
...cheaper than competitor price		
...market price		

(8 marks)

(d) Would the proposed policy of pricing at 25% margin ensure that all new products at least break even? (You can assume that the costs are correctly calculated.)

[▼]

Picklist:

Yes
No

(1 mark)

(e) Explain your answer to (d).

(2 marks)

Task 4 (20 marks)

Louise Harding, the Finance Director, is preparing a presentation for the Board of Directors. She has asked you to complete a comparative 'score card' of key financial ratios which she will use as part of her presentation.

Relevant data has been extracted from the last two years' accounts. These extracts do not include the results of Merville Ltd.

Extracts from accounts of SL Products Ltd	Year ended 31 December 20X2 £000	Year ended 31 December 20X3 £000
Sales revenue	20,900	21,200
Cost of sales	15,144	15,609
Profit from operations	470	328
Assets		
Non-current assets	4,234	3,701
Inventories	3,908	4,579
Trade receivables	3,032	3,384
Cash and equivalents	6	8
Total	**11,180**	**11,672**
Equity and Liabilities		
Equity	5,550	5,600
Non-current liabilities	1,400	1,600
Trade payables	3,730	4,020
Bank overdraft	260	302
Tax liabilities	240	150
Total	**11,180**	**11,672**

(a) Complete the scorecard by calculating the missing ratios.

SL Products Ltd Scorecard	Year ended 31 Dec 20X2	Year ended 31 Dec 20X3
Profitability and gearing (correct to 1 dp):		
Gross profit %	27.5 %	%
Operating profit %	2.2 %	%
Return on capital employed	6.8 %	%
Gearing	20.1 %	%
Liquidity ratios (correct to 1 dp):		
Current ratio	1.6:1	:1
Acid test/quick ratio	0.7:1	:1
Working capital days (correct to nearest day):		
Inventory holding period	94 days	days
Trade receivables collection period	53 days	days
Trade payables payment period	90 days	days
Working capital cycle	57 days	days

(10 marks)

(b) Select the ONE correct observation about each aspect of business performance below.

Profitability

	✓
Profitability has dipped slightly, due to poor sales.	
The profitability ratios give serious cause for concern. The small increase in sales revenue has failed to compensate for increased cost of sales and operating expenses.	
The ratios give mixed messages. Some have improved and some have deteriorated. Further investigation is required.	

(2 marks)

Gearing

	✓
The increased gearing ratio only reflects the fact that an extra loan has been taken out.	
The increased gearing ratio shows that equity has increased at a greater rate than non-current liabilities.	
The increased gearing ratio shows that the company has become more risky.	

(2 marks)

Liquidity

	✓
Both ratios have deteriorated which indicates that the company is less solvent.	
Both ratios have improved, indicating there are no concerns about the company's liquidity or solvency.	
The improvement in the liquidity ratios indicates that the company is succeeding in managing its cash flows.	

(2 marks)

Working capital

	✓
The longer working capital cycle indicates the company is insolvent.	
The shorter working capital cycle indicates the company can repay some of its long-term liabilities.	
The change in the working capital cycle requires urgent investigation.	

(2 marks)

Overall performance

	✓
Profitability has declined in 20X3, mainly due to competitive pressures. However, the gearing and liquidity measures show an improving financial position.	
20X3 has been a bad year. Profitability has declined and finances are coming under serious pressure.	
Steady progress has been made in 20X3. The ratios show that the company is being better managed.	

(2 marks)

Task 5 (20 marks)

This task contains parts (a) to (e).

(a) Identify whether each of the following statements in relation to internal controls is true or false. **(5 marks)**

Statement	True	False
One of the purposes of internal controls is to protect the accounting system from systemic weaknesses, fraudulent activities and human error.		
A robust internal control system increases the risk of loss but reduces the risk of fraud.		
Internal controls ensure that a company is working to meet its strategic objectives.		
The internal control system is a combination of the board of directors and the internal audit department.		
Internal controls can be used to ensure ethical standards are met within an organisation.		

You have been asked to carry out a review of SL Products Ltd's purchases order processing procedure and make recommendations for improvement.

You have interviewed the Finance Director (Louise Harding), the Production Director (Colin Smith) and the Purchasing Manager (Tony Clark). Your findings are below.

- Suppliers are identified and contacted direct by individuals who require the goods or service in question.
- All purchases on credit are recorded on an official purchase order by that individual. The order states the price and delivery date, if known.
- All departments are provided with books of pre-numbered order forms. These books can be obtained from the stationery store.
- Capital expenditure orders must be raised and signed by Louise Harding.
- Other orders must be signed by the individual placing the order.
- New suppliers are given a trade reference and banking details by Tony Clark, who also requests credit terms. These are subject to negotiation, though the company's preferred terms are to pay 60 days from the end of the month in which delivery takes place.

You are required to identify four features of these procedures: one strength; one weakness; one threat and one opportunity. Do not use the same feature more than once.

(b) Identify a strength in these procedures. Explain how the business benefits from the strength.

(3 marks)

(c) Identify a weakness in these procedures. Explain how the weakness damages the business and suggest a remedy.

(4 marks)

(d) Identify an opportunity to improve the procedures to the benefit of the business.

(4 marks)

(e) Identify a threat in these procedures that could damage the business and suggest an action that would reduce the risk.

(4 marks)

BPP PRACTICE ASSESSMENT 1
LEVEL 4 SYNOPTIC ASSESSMENT

ANSWERS

Level 4 Synoptic Assessment
BPP practice assessment 1: answers

Task 1 (20 marks)

(a) The statutory duty to report whether SL Products Ltd's financial statements show a true and fair view is that of [the company's auditors].

(2 marks)

(b)

	✓
Prepare a journal to record the necessary reversal of the purchase invoice	
Prepare a debit note and send it to the supplier	
Advise the Accounts Payable Clerk of the omission	✓
Advise Liz Hall, the Accounts Payable Clerk, to reverse the relevant invoice from the purchases day book	

(2 marks)

(c)

VAT on a sales invoice posted to sales instead of VAT control	Would not be detected
A sales invoice credited to the customer's account	Would be detected
A sales invoice posted to the wrong customer account	Would not be detected
A batch of purchase invoices posted to the sales ledger control account	Would be detected
A pricing error in a sales invoice	Would not be detected

(5 marks)

(d)

	✓
98765432	
acsystem	
1jan2000	
?win121#	✓

(2 marks)

(e) [Confidentiality]

[You must refuse to share any information]

(4 marks)

(f)

Wastage reports from the production line	Operational
Inventory turnover reports	Tactical
Inventory level reports	Operational
Future demand estimates for the next 12 months	Strategic
Analysis of competitor's products and their market positioning	Strategic

(5 marks)

Task 2 (20 marks)

(a) Match the appropriate category of internal controls to each description **(5 marks)**

Description	Category of internal control
Checking the VAT calculation on an invoice before processing	Arithmetic
Review of the daily unallocated cash report from the receivables ledger by the financial controller	Management
Preparation of the supplier payment run by the cashier, rather than the purchase ledger clerk	Segregation of duties
Each employee has a written job description and a clear chain of management	Organisational
Two factor authentication is required to access the cloud accounting software	Physical

(b) Marking guide: A maximum of 5 weaknesses and the potential problems, with each weakness awarded 1 mark and each problem 2 marks (to a maximum of 3 marks).

No.	(i) Weakness	(ii) Potential problem
1	Cynthia Moss appears to have very little involvement in day-to-day sales, apart from negotiating terms with new customers.	Failures in the system and system abuses could go unnoticed.
2	The procedures do not include any mention of checking that goods of the correct category and standard have been despatched.	If this is not happening the company could be sending out sub-standard goods.
3	Orders can be taken without agreeing a price.	The company is in a weak position to negotiate price after the goods or service have been despatched.

No.	(i) Weakness	(ii) Potential problem
4	Lack of authorisation of new accounts.	There should be a policy for deciding on whether to offer credit at all. Potential for fraud through collusion with customers.
5	The terms agreed by Ray Massey are not countersigned.	Potential for fraud through collusion with customers.
6	Only one signature is required on most orders.	Potential for fraud through collusion with customers.
7	Matthew Tunnock checks, clears and arranges payment of invoices.	Potential for fraud through collusion with customers.
8	Matthew Tunnock controls all aspects of sales accounting.	Potential for fraud.
9	Receipts are only monitored and posted once a week.	Increases the opportunity for teeming and lading, and means a bad service will be given to customers if they ring with a query.
10	No counter-signatory required for credit notes.	Potential for fraud through collusion with customers.

(15 marks)

Note. Only **five** weaknesses were required.

Task 3 (20 marks)

(a) Match the cost type to each description. **(5 marks)**

Description	Cost type
Purchases of non-current assets or the improvement of the earning capability of non-current assets	Capital expenditure
Cost which is fixed for a short range and then increases in steps	Semi-fixed cost
Costs that can be specifically attributed to a cost unit	Direct cost
Costs that change directly in line with any change in activity level	Variable cost
The total of all direct costs	Prime cost

(b)

Prices for new products	£ per unit	
	AB	**CD**
Materials and labour	72.00	45.00
Variable production overheads (W1)	14.40	9.00
Fixed production overheads	6.00	3.00
Other fixed overheads	6.30	3.60
Total cost	98.70	60.60
Price at 25% margin (W2)	131.60	80.80

Workings

(1) 20% × materials and labour
(2) Total cost ÷ 0.75

(4 marks)

(c)

	AB £	**CD £**
Marginal cost per unit	86.40	54.00
Annual contribution if price level is...		
...price at 25% margin	7,910	6,700
...cheaper than competitor price	11,580	5,500
...market price	11,990	6,300

(8 marks)

(d) Yes

(1 mark)

(e) The 25% margin prices are based on full cost because the company operates a full overhead recovery pricing model. This means that, at the 25% margin price, each product breaks even by covering its fixed costs, then makes a positive contribution to profit.

(2 marks)

Task 4 (20 marks)

(a)

SL Products Ltd Scorecard	Year ended 31 Dec 20X2	Year ended 31 Dec 20X3
Profitability and gearing (correct to 1 dp):		
Gross profit %	27.5%	**26.4** %
Operating profit %	2.2%	**1.5** %
Return on capital employed	6.8%	**4.6** %
Gearing	20.1%	**22.2** %
Liquidity ratios (correct to 1 dp):		
Current ratio	1.6:1	**1.8** :1
Acid test/quick ratio	0.7:1	**0.8** :1
Working capital days (correct to nearest day):		
Inventory holding period	94 days	**107** days
Trade receivables collection period	53 days	**58** days
Trade payables payment period	90 days	**94** days
Working capital cycle	57 days	**71** days

(10 marks)

(b) Profitability

	✓
Profitability has dipped slightly, due to poor sales.	
The profitability ratios give serious cause for concern. The small increase in sales revenue has failed to compensate for increased cost of sales and operating expenses.	✓
The ratios give mixed messages. Some have improved and some have deteriorated. Further investigation is required.	

(2 marks)

Gearing

	✓
The increased gearing ratio only reflects the fact that an extra loan has been taken out.	
The increased gearing ratio shows that equity has increased at a greater rate than non-current liabilities.	
The increased gearing ratio shows that the company has become more risky.	✓

(2 marks)

Liquidity

	✓
Both ratios have deteriorated which indicates that the company is less solvent.	
Both ratios have improved, indicating there are no concerns about the company's liquidity or solvency.	
The improvement in the liquidity ratios indicates that the company is succeeding in managing its cash flows.	✓

(2 marks)

Working capital

	✓
The longer working capital cycle indicates the company is insolvent.	
The shorter working capital cycle indicates the company can repay some of its long-term liabilities.	
The change in the working capital cycle requires urgent investigation.	✓

(2 marks)

Overall performance

	✓
Profitability has declined in 20X3, mainly due to competitive pressures. However, the gearing and liquidity measures show an improving financial position.	
20X3 has been a bad year. Profitability has declined and finances are coming under serious pressure.	✓
Steady progress has been made in 20X3. The ratios show that the company is being better managed.	

(2 marks)

Task 5 (20 marks)

(a) Identify whether each of the following statements in relation to internal controls is true or false. (5 marks)

Statement	True	False
One of the purposes of internal controls is to protect the accounting system from systemic weaknesses, fraudulent activities and human error.	X	
A robust internal control system increases the risk of loss but reduces the risk of fraud.		X
Internal controls ensure that a company is working to meet its strategic objectives.	X	
The internal control system is a combination of the board of directors and the internal audit department.		X
Internal controls can be used to ensure ethical standards are met within an organisation.	X	

Note. The question only requires one strength and one weakness. Additional items are provided here to illustrate the range of possible answers.

(b) **(i)** The highest value items – for capital expenditure – require senior management authority before being ordered, and all purchases on credit require proper purchase orders. Staff understand therefore that proper procedures must be followed before items can be purchased, which reduces the risk of unnecessary items being bought by the company or that staff purchase items for themselves at the company's expense.

(ii) A coherent approach is taken towards negotiating credit terms with suppliers, which benefits the company's cash flow and planning.

(3 marks)

(c) **(i)** It appears items can be purchased from suppliers without a price or delivery time having been agreed upon. This introduces unnecessary uncertainty into the company's operations, costs and cash flows. The remedy is that no purchase orders may be raised without an agreed price being stated on them.

(ii) There is no security over the purchase order forms, so in theory any staff member or other person may obtain a form and purchase items to the account of SL Products Ltd. This means the company may be liable to pay for items it has not received or does not want. The remedy is to ensure that purchases can only be recorded and paid for if the purchase invoice when received can be matched to a purchase order.

(iii) Outside of capital expenditure there is no need for countersignature to indicate higher authority, and no cash limit on an individual purchase. In theory this could result in large amounts being spent inappropriately.

(4 marks)

(d) The involvement of Tony Clark, the Purchasing Manager, with suppliers seems to focus only on how long the company can take to pay. There is an opportunity to expand his role significantly to: (1) identify and quality assure suppliers independently of user departments; (2) guide and authorise departments in their purchases; and (3) negotiate prices, delivery terms and discounts with existing and new suppliers.

(4 marks)

(e) The lack of supervision and co-ordination of purchasing suggests that optimum purchasing quantities and careful inventory management are completely overlooked. This could leave the company with significant amounts of inventory that it does not need and cannot use. As well as making a loss on these items, the business will also suffer cash flow problems. There is an urgent need for a more coherent approach to purchasing, especially but not only for Production, so that the company achieves a balance between having inventory when it is needed and having too high a level that drains its resources.

(4 marks)

BPP PRACTICE ASSESSMENT 2
LEVEL 4 SYNOPTIC ASSESSMENT

Time allowed: 3 hours

PRACTICE ASSESSMENT 2

Level 4 Synoptic Assessment
BPP practice assessment 2

This practice assessment is based on the same scenario as AAT's practice assessment, SL Products Ltd. See pages 113–117 for the relevant pre-reading material.

Task 1 (20 marks)

(a) Complete the following statement.

The statutory duty to maintain a public record of information about SL Products Ltd is that of [▼].

Picklist:

Companies House
Sue Hughes, the chief accountant
the company's directors
the company's auditors

At SL Products Ltd the task of preparing the payroll is performed by Jane Patel, Payroll Clerk. Within the company line managers authorise staff timesheets, and Hina Khan (General Accounts Clerk and cashier) processes payments to employees. Colin Smith, Production Director, discovers that the timesheet of the production supervisor, Naseem Hadid, has been omitted from the weekly payroll.

(2 marks)

(b) What is the correct action for Colin Smith to take?

	✓
Instruct Hina Khan to make an immediate bank transfer to Naseem	
Advise Jane Patel of the omission	
Prepare a journal to record Naseem's gross pay	
Write out a cheque for Naseem	

(2 marks)

(c) Jane Patel, the Payroll Clerk, has asked you to show whether the following errors would be detected by clearing the wages control account.

Ten hours pay paid to J. Utley instead of T. Utley	▼
Gross pay credited to an expense account	▼
Payment of PAYE to the pension administrator rather than HMRC	▼
Miscalculation of employer's National Insurance	▼
A transposition error in the net pay authority given to BACS	▼

Picklist:

Would be detected
Would not be detected

(5 marks)

You have been asked to ensure the correct controls are in place to validate data input to SL Products Ltd's accounting system.

(d) Which of the following types of control are relevant?

	✓
System controls	
Physical access controls	
Integrity controls	

(2 marks)

Your duties at SL Products Ltd include preparing the consolidated accounts. Sue Hughes, the chief accountant, is aware that the company's most recent results are not good. She has instructed you to ensure that, when valuing inventory, the highest possible valuation is placed on each item whether or not this is in line with IAS 2 *Inventories.*

(e) Answer the following questions.

Which of your fundamental principles is threatened by this request?

	▼

Picklist:

Confidentiality
Integrity
Objectivity

What action should you take?

	▼

Picklist:

You must comply with IAS 2 *Inventories*
You must comply with Sue's instruction
You must notify the National Crime Agency of Sue's instruction

(4 marks)

(f) Identify whether each of the following control activities is an integrity, system, physical access or management security control. Select your answer using the picklist (answers may be used more than once).

Keypad entry to the accounting office	▼
User access restrictions to areas of the accountancy software	▼
Review of the log file for access to areas of the accountancy system by the Financial Director	▼

Picklist:

Integrity control
Physical access control
System control

(3 marks)

(g) Which TWO of the following statements reflects a tall organisational structure?

	✓
Management have a wide span of control	
Structure is highly dependent on hierarchy	
Management do a wide variety of tasks within the organisation	
Management have a smaller team, with clear, strict boundaries and tasks set	

(2 marks)

Task 2 (20 marks)

This task contains parts (a) and (b)

(a) You have found a number of systemic weaknesses in the internal controls in SL Products Ltd's accounting system. Identify what, if any, effect each one will have on the company's reported profit.

Systemic weakness	No effect on reported profit ✓	Understatement of reported profit ✓	Overstatement of reported profit ✓
Omitting sales		✓	
Understating the allowance for doubtful debts			✓
Overstating assets	✓		
Understating expenses			✓
Writing off valid debts as irrecoverable		✓	

(5 marks)

You have been asked to review the adequacy of the controls in SL Products Ltd's payroll procedures. Your review has established the following information.

The company operates an integrated accounting system which includes a payroll accounting module. Sue Hughes, the Chief Accountant, is responsible for managing payroll activities. Jane Patel, the Payroll Clerk, performs day-to-day payroll tasks.

Warehouse staff are required to be paid an hourly rate. Staff members complete a timecard each week which is submitted directly to finance, including any overtime worked. Overtime rates vary depending on the employee's contract.

Other staff, including sales staff and the finance team are paid a monthly salary according to their employment contract. Sales staff can receive a bonus for meeting sales targets set by sales director, Cynthia Moss. Cynthia emails Jane to let her know if any sales team member should receive a bonus each month, but Jane needs to do the calculations of the bonus amount.

Jane Patel's responsibilities include:

- Maintaining standing data on employees
- Recording each employee's hours at work where this information is relevant and available
- Calculating gross pay and deductions
- Preparing the wages control account
- Preparing the BACS payments each month to employees and HMRC
- Reconciling total pay and deductions in the wages control account

Employee details, including wage and salary levels, overtime rates and sales bonus entitlements are maintained by the HR department but relevant finance department members are also able to update these details.

Once a month, after the payroll and its associated payments are complete, Sue Hughes reviews total payroll cost against budget and investigates unexpected variances.

(b) (i) Identify FIVE systemic weaknesses with the company's procedures, including its internal controls, that underpin its payroll practices and systems. (5 marks)

(ii) For each weakness explain two potential problems they could cause the company. (10 marks)

Note. You are **NOT** required to make recommendations to change the procedures.

No.	Weakness	Potential problem
1		
2		
3		
4		
5		

Task 3 (20 marks)

This task contains parts (a) to (c).

(a) Identify whether the following statements in relation to budgetary control are TRUE or FALSE.

Statement	True	False
Fixed budget are budgets that are set at the end of the period to check that the financial statements are reasonable.		
Information about the budgetary control system is relayed to participants via feedback and feedforward systems.		
A flexible budget has two uses within an organisation: planning and control.		

Statement	True	False
Before flexing a budget, costs need to be categorised as fixed or variable		
Variances are calculated by adding the actual result to the flexed budget figure.		

(5 marks)

You have been given the following information for the manufacture of units of HW by SL Products Ltd for the month just ended.

	Budget		Actual	
Production (units of HW)		48,000		50,400
Direct materials	19,200 kg	£230,400	20,600 kg	£252,350

Louise Harding, the Finance Director, has asked you to write a note to help in the training of a junior accounting technician. The notes are to explain the calculation of the total direct material variance and how this variance can be split into a price variance and a usage variance.

(b) Explain the total direct material variance and how it can be split into a price variance and usage variance. Use calculations to illustrate your explanation.

(10 marks)

Sue Hughes, the Chief Accountant, has prepared the following budgetary control report for the product QR produced by SL Products Ltd, together with the variances calculated below.

	Budget		Actual	
Production (units)		5,100		5,500
Direct materials	15,500 kg	£57,320	15,600 kg	£54,600
Direct labour	10,200 hours	£112,200	12,100 hours	£139,150
Fixed overheads		£97,500		£96,300
Total cost		£267,020		£290,050

Variances	Amount £
Direct materials price	3,090 F
Direct materials usage	4,130 F
Direct labour rate	6,050 A
Direct labour efficiency	Not yet calculated
Fixed overhead expenditure	Not yet calculated

SL Products Ltd normally prepares an operating statement under standard absorption costing principles but Louise Harding, the Finance Director, has asked you to prepare an operating statement under standard marginal costing principles.

(c) Place each variance into the correct column (favourable or adverse) and complete the table.

			£
Budgeted variable cost for actual production			
Budgeted fixed cost			
Total budgeted cost for actual production			
Variance	**Favourable £**	**Adverse £**	
Direct materials price			
Direct materials usage	4,130		
Direct labour rate			
Direct labour efficiency			
Fixed overhead expenditure			
Fixed overhead volume			
Total variance			9,730
Actual cost of actual production			

(5 marks)

Task 4 (20 marks)

Louise Harding, the Finance Director, is preparing a presentation for the Board of Directors. She has asked you to complete a comparative 'score card' of key financial ratios which she will use as part of her presentation.

Relevant data has been extracted from the last two years' accounts. These extracts do not include the results of Merville Ltd.

Extracts from accounts of SL Products Ltd	Year ended 31 December 20X3 £000	Year ended 31 December 20X4 £000
Sales revenue	21,200	23,900
Cost of sales	15,609	15,904
Profit from operations	328	508
Assets		
Non-current assets	3,701	4,715
Inventories	4,579	3,197
Trade receivables	3,384	2,559
Cash and equivalents	8	38
Total	**11,672**	**10,509**
Equity and Liabilities		
Equity	5,600	6,200
Non-current liabilities	1,600	1,000
Trade payables	4,020	3,099
Bank overdraft	302	0
Tax liabilities	150	210
Total	**11,672**	**10,509**

(a) Complete the scorecard by calculating the missing ratios for the year ended 31 December 20X4.

SL Products Ltd Scorecard	Year ended 31 Dec 20X3	Year ended 31 Dec 20X4
Profitability and gearing (correct to 1 dp):		
Gross profit %	26.4%	%
Operating profit %	1.5%	%
Return on capital employed	4.6%	%
Gearing	22.2%	%
Liquidity ratios (correct to 1 dp):		
Current ratio	1.8:1	:1
Acid test/quick ratio	0.8:1	:1
Working capital days (correct to nearest day):		
Inventory holding period	107 days	days
Trade receivables collection period	58 days	days
Trade payables payment period	94 days	days
Working capital cycle	71 days	days

(10 marks)

(b) Select the ONE correct observation about each aspect of business performance below.

Profitability

	✓
Profitability has improved due to improved sales and reduced costs.	
The profitability ratios have improved due to increased sales, but cost control is still a problem.	
The ratios give mixed messages. Some have improved and some have deteriorated. Further investigation is required.	

(2 marks)

Gearing

	✓
The reduced gearing ratio reflects that equity has partially replaced lending in the company's financial structure.	
The level of gearing is not related to the company's profitability.	
The increased gearing ratio shows that the company has become more risky.	

(2 marks)

Liquidity

	✓
Both ratios have deteriorated which indicates that the company is less solvent.	
Both ratios have improved, indicating there are no concerns about the company's liquidity or solvency.	
Comparing the liquidity ratios with last year's tells us little about the company's solvency.	

(2 marks)

Working capital

	✓
The longer working capital cycle indicates the company is insolvent.	
The shorter working capital cycle indicates the company has addressed some solvency issues that appeared in 20X3.	
The change in the working capital cycle requires urgent investigation.	

(2 marks)

Overall performance and position

	✓
The company has a new shareholder whose cash has been used to invest in improving profitability and reducing financial risk.	
Steady progress has been made in 20X4, but profitability has declined and the company remains risky.	
The company continues to perform badly and is in danger of insolvency.	

(2 marks)

Task 5 (20 marks)

This task contains parts (a) to (d).

(a) Identify whether each of the following actions are examples of FRAUD or ERROR.

Actions	Fraud	Error
Theft of equipment from the company warehouse		
Miscalculation of the VAT on a customer invoice		
Misclassifying a bank loan as equity to improve gearing to avoid default		
Deliberate underpayment of PAYE to HMRC		
Money laundering		

(5 marks)

In the last year SL Products Ltd's subsidiary, Merville Ltd, has found serious weaknesses in each of its three main transaction streams which arise from particular uncontrolled risks. Its finance director has asked you for advice on how to avoid or reduce these risks.

(b) You are required to identify ONE control objective and ONE control activity for each risk.

Transaction stream	Risk	Control objective	Control activity
Payroll	Company is fined for non-compliance with PAYE regulations		
Sales	Company charges for goods in error and loses custom		
Purchasing	Company pays more than once for the same goods and the supplier does not correct the mistake		

(6 marks)

Sue Hughes, the Chief Accountant, presents you with Merville Ltd's monthly operating report. The original budget has been flexed to the level of actual activity, and variances calculated.

You are told that:

- Material, labour and distribution costs are variable.
- Power is a semi-variable cost. The fixed element is budgeted at £5,300 per month.
- Premises costs are stepped, and budgeted to double at every 75,000 units of monthly production (at this level the company hires a second workshop at a daily all-inclusive rate).
- Depreciation, marketing and administration costs are fixed.
- The company does not use full absorption costing.

Monthly operating report

Original budget		Flexed budget	Actual	Variance Fav/(Adv)
74,200	Sales volume (units)		80,000	
£		£	£	£
534,240	Sales revenue	576,000	581,400	5,400
	Costs			
192,920	Materials	208,000	211,520	–3,520
200,340	Labour	216,000	221,300	–5,300
29,680	Distribution	32,000	33,100	–1,100
27,560	Power	29,300	29,150	150
10,000	Premises costs	20,000	10,000	10,000
3,650	Depreciation	3,650	3,600	50
32,500	Marketing	32,500	33,400	–900
10,670	Administration	10,670	9,980	690
507,320	Total	552,120	552,050	70
26,920	Operating profit/(loss)	23,880	29,350	5,470

Write an email to Sue Hughes to explain:

(c) The main factors that led to the actual profit being higher than the original budgeted profit.

(5 marks)

(d) How improved internal controls can assist in controlling the adverse variances.

(4 marks)

BPP PRACTICE ASSESSMENT 2
LEVEL 4 SYNOPTIC ASSESSMENT

ANSWERS

Level 4 Synoptic Assessment
BPP practice assessment 2: answers

Task 1 (20 marks)

(a) The statutory duty to maintain a public record of information about SL Products Ltd is that of [Companies House] .

(2 marks)

(b)

	✓
Instruct Hina Khan to make an immediate bank transfer to Naseem	
Advise Jane Patel of the omission	✓
Prepare a journal to record Naseem's gross pay	
Write out a cheque for Naseem	

(2 marks)

(c)

Ten hours pay paid to J. Utley instead of T. Utley	Would not be detected
Gross pay credited to an expense account	Would be detected
Payment of PAYE to the pension administrator rather than HMRC	Would not be detected
Miscalculation of employer's National Insurance	Would not be detected
A transposition error in the net pay authority given to BACS	Would be detected

(5 marks)

(d)

	✓
System controls	
Physical access controls	
Integrity controls	✓

(2 marks)

(e) [Integrity]

[You must comply with IAS 2 *Inventories*]

(4 marks)

(f)

Keypad entry to the accounting office	Physical access control
User access restrictions to areas of the accountancy software	Integrity control
Review of the log file for access of areas of the accountancy system by the Financial Director	System control

(3 marks)

(g)

	✓
Management have a wide span of control	
Structure is highly dependent on hierarchy	✓
Management do a wide variety of tasks within the organisation	
Management have a smaller team, with clear, strict boundaries and tasks set.	✓

(2 marks)

Task 2 (20 marks)

(a)

Systemic weakness	No effect on reported profit ✓	Understatement of reported profit ✓	Overstatement of reported profit ✓
Omitting sales		✓	
Understating the allowance for doubtful debts			✓
Overstating assets	✓		
Understating expenses			✓
Writing off valid debts as irrecoverable		✓	

(b) Marking guide: A maximum of 5 weaknesses and the potential problems, with each weakness awarded 1 mark and each problem 2 marks (to a maximum of 3 marks).

No.	Weakness	Potential problem
1	There is a lack of management supervision of the day-to-day payroll activities.	Errors or fraud could take place without detection. Jane might feel unsupported in her role without proper supervisory support.
2	Lack of segregation of duties	Jane has control over the whole payroll process. She could manipulate the payroll for personal gain without any form of challenge or oversight.
3	Lack of authorisation of warehouse staff hours	Warehouse staff submit their timecards directly to finance without these being checked/authorised by a supervisor. There is a risk that the wrong hours could be recorded leading to the wrong payment being made.
4	Calculation of sales bonuses	Jane is told which members of the sales team are entitled to a bonus, but she does the calculations herself. There is a risk she could miss a payment or calculate the payment incorrectly.
5	Lack of control over standing data	Members of the finance department can change the standing data on employees. There is a risk that changes could be made fraudulently or in error which could lead to financial loss for the company. There is also a risk that this might lead to the wrong payments to HMRC.
6	Payments made without checks or authorisation	Payroll payments are made to employees and HMRC without any management authorisation. There is a risk that incorrect payments could be made. There is a risk that payments that should have been made are omitted in error.
7	Lack of management oversight	The chief accountant only reviews the total payroll cost against budget. There are no other management checks over the payroll process which may result in fraud or error. There is a risk of non-compliance with HMRC due to incorrect payments.

(15 marks)

Note. Only **five** weaknesses were required.

Task 3 (20 marks)

(a) Identify whether the following statements in relation to budgetary control are TRUE or FALSE.

Statement	True	False
Fixed budget are budgets that are set at the end of the period to check that the financial statements are reasonable.		X
Information about the budgetary control system is relayed to participants via feedback and feedforward systems.	X	
A flexible budget has two uses within an organisation: planning and control.	X	
Before flexing a budget, costs need to be categorised as fixed or variable	X	
Variances are calculated by adding the actual result to the flexed budget figure.		X

(5 marks)

(b) The total direct material variance compares the **flexed budget cost** for materials with the **actual cost** incurred. The flexed budget is the total budgeted cost of materials for the actual production of 50,400 units. It is not useful simply to calculate the variance as £21,950 adverse by comparing the actual cost of £252,350 with the budgeted cost of £230,400, because the two figures are based on different volumes of activity.

Flexing the budget calculates the **quantity of materials** which we would expect to use to produce the **actual production** achieved. If 19,200 kgs are required to make 48,000 units then 0.4 kg is required to make 1 unit (19,200/48,000). To make 50400 units we therefore require 20,160 kgs (50,400 × 0.4 kg). We expect each kg to cost £12 (£230,400/19,200). Therefore we expect that making 50,400 units would require 20,160 kilograms at a cost of £12 per kilogram, that is £241,920.

We now compare the **flexed budget cost** of £241,920 with the **actual cost** (£252,350) to produce the total material variance of £10,430. This variance is adverse because the **actual cost was greater than the flexed budgeted cost**.

The total variance can be split into two elements:

- The variance due to the price paid per kilogram being different from what we expected. This is the material price variance.
- The variance due to the quantity of material used per unit of production being different from what we expected. This is the material usage variance.

The expected cost of the 20,600 kilograms used is £247,200 (20,600 × £12).

Price variance

We calculate the price variance by comparing the **actual cost** of the 20,600 kilograms (£252,350) with the **expected cost** (£247,200). The difference or variance is £5,150. This variance is adverse because the **actual cost is greater than the expected cost**.

Material usage variance

We calculate the material usage variance by calculating the quantity of materials which we would expect to use to produce the actual volume of production. 50,400 units were produced and the expected quantity of materials to make these units is 20,160 kilograms. If we compare this with the actual quantity used of 20,600 kilograms we get an adverse variance of 440 kilograms, since we used more than we expected. This needs to be **valued at the**

expected cost of £12 per kilogram. The adverse usage variance is £5,280 (440 × £12). The usage variance is always valued at the expected cost (the standard cost) because the price variance has already been isolated.

Total materials variance

Together the materials price and usage variances reconcile back to the total materials variance. The price variance of £5,150 adverse plus the £5,280 adverse usage variance explains the total variance of £10,430.

(10 marks)

(c)

			£
Budgeted variable cost for actual production			182,820
Budgeted fixed cost			97,500
Total budgeted cost for actual production			280,320
Variance	**Favourable £**	**Adverse £**	
Direct materials price	3,090		
Direct materials usage	4,130		
Direct labour rate		6,050	
Direct labour efficiency		12,100	
Fixed overhead expenditure	1,200		
Fixed overhead volume			
Total variance	8,420	18,150	9,730
Actual cost of actual production			290,050

(5 marks)

Workings

Budgeted variable cost per unit = (£57,320 + £112,200)/5,100 units = £33.24

Budgeted variable cost for actual production = 5,500 units × £33.24 = £182,820

Total budgeted cost for actual production = £182,820 + £97,500 (fixed costs)
= £280,320

Direct labour efficiency variance

5,500 units should have taken (× 10,200/5,100 hours)	11,000 hrs
But did take	12,100 hrs
	1,100 hrs (A)
At standard rate (£112,200/10,200)	× £11.00
Efficiency variance	£12,100 (A)

Fixed overhead expenditure variance = £97,500 – £96,300 = £1,200. Actual £1,200 lower than budgeted, so favourable.

Task 4 (20 marks)

(a)

SL Products Ltd Scorecard	Year ended 31 Dec 20X3	Year ended 31 Dec 20X4
Profitability and gearing (correct to 1 dp):		
Gross profit %	26.4%	**33.5** %
Operating profit %	1.5%	**2.1** %
Return on capital employed	4.6%	**7.1** %
Gearing	22.2%	**13.9** %
Liquidity ratios (correct to 1 dp):		
Current ratio	1.8:1	**1.8** :1
Acid test/quick ratio	0.8:1	**0.8** :1
Working capital days (correct to nearest day):		
Inventory holding period	107 days	**73** days
Trade receivables collection period	58 days	**39** days
Trade payables payment period	94 days	**71** days
Working capital cycle	71 days	**41** days

(10 marks)

(b) Profitability

	✓
Profitability has improved due to improved sales and reduced costs.	✓
The profitability ratios have improved due to increased sales, but cost control is still a problem.	
The ratios give mixed messages. Some have improved and some have deteriorated. Further investigation is required.	

(2 marks)

Gearing

	✓
The reduced gearing ratio reflects that equity has partially replaced lending in the company's financial structure.	✓
The level of gearing is not related to the company's profitability.	
The increased gearing ratio shows that the company has become more risky.	

(2 marks)

Liquidity

	✓
Both ratios have deteriorated which indicates that the company is less solvent.	
Both ratios have improved, indicating there are no concerns about the company's liquidity or solvency.	
Comparing the liquidity ratios with last year's tells us little about the company's solvency.	✓

(2 marks)

Working capital

	✓
The longer working capital cycle indicates the company is insolvent.	
The shorter working capital cycle indicates the company has addressed some solvency issues that appeared in 20X3.	✓
The change in the working capital cycle requires urgent investigation.	

(2 marks)

Overall performance and position

	✓
The company has a new shareholder whose cash has been used to invest in improving profitability and reducing financial risk.	✓
Steady progress has been made in 20X4, but profitability has declined and the company remains risky.	
The company continues to perform badly and is in danger of insolvency.	

(2 marks)

Task 5 (20 marks)

(a) Identify whether each of the following actions are examples of FRAUD or ERROR.

Actions	Fraud	Error
Theft of equipment from the company warehouse	X	
Miscalculation of the VAT on a customer invoice		X
Misclassifying a bank loan as equity to improve gearing to avoid default	X	
Deliberate underpayment of PAYE to HMRC	X	
Money laundering	X	

(5 marks)

(b)

Transaction stream	Risk	Control objective	Control activity
Payroll	Company is fined for non-compliance with PAYE regulations	Ensure all deductions have been properly calculated and authorised	Check calculation and authorisation of all deductions Maintain separate records for each employee Reconcile total pay and deductions in wages control account regularly
Sales	Company charges for goods in error and loses custom	Only invoice goods that have been sent out	Ask customers to sign despatch notes as proof of receipt Prepare sales invoices from signed despatch notes and sales orders
Purchasing	Company pays more than once for the same goods and the supplier does not correct the mistake	Only pay for liabilities once	Record payments promptly in the cash book and ledger. Only pay supplier invoices that match checked GRNs

(6 marks)

(c) The key factor leading to the actual profit being higher than the originally budgeted profit is the increase in sales volume achieved. Actual sales were 80,000 units compared to an original budget of 74,200 units, an 8% increase. Also helping is an increase in the sales price achieved, budgeted to be £534,240/74,200 = £7.20 per unit, but actually achieved at £581,400/80,000 = £7.27, a 0.9% increase.

The second reason for the higher than budgeted profit is the £10,000 favourable variance on premises costs. A second workshop was budgeted but the company has managed with one workshop, presumably because opening inventory of finished goods was sufficient to achieve sales of 80,000 units without producing more than 75,000 units in the year.

Some costs, eg materials and labour, report adverse variances so tend to reduce the profit achieved. Others, eg administration, report a favourable variance so increase the profit achieved.

However, it is the favourable increase in sales volume and premises variances that are the main factors in explaining the increase in profit.

(5 marks)

(d) It is possible that there may have been errors in the prices charged by suppliers for materials and distribution. Internal controls over the use of price lists when ordering should be checked. There may have been errors in processing and recording purchases underlying the costs, or there may have been poor purchasing procedures so that the best deal on prices was not secured.

As far as labour costs are concerned there may be operational reasons, such as the use of overtime, for the variance on labour costs. However, there may have been poor control of time, mis-recording of time, and deliberate or careless overpayment of employees. Authorisation and management controls over payroll costs should be reviewed.

(4 marks)

BPP PRACTICE ASSESSMENT 3
LEVEL 4 SYNOPTIC ASSESSMENT

Time allowed: 3 hours

PRACTICE ASSESSMENT 3

BPP LEARNING MEDIA

Level 4 Synoptic Assessment
BPP practice assessment 3

This practice assessment is based on the same scenario as AAT's live assessment, Argent Electric Motors Ltd for assessments from 2 October 2023. See page 147 for the relevant pre-reading material, and the latest version can be obtained from www.aat.org.uk

Task 1 (20 marks)

(a) Complete the following statement.

AEM Ltd has a [▼] accounting function. The accounting function will produce [▼] information such as budgets to help the directors with planning, decision making, controlling and [▼].

Picklist:

centralised
decentralised
financial
management
reporting to shareholders
performance measurement

(3 marks)

AEM Ltd are considering offering the supply and installation of electric car charging ports. Chris Davis, the financial controller, is trying to build a budget for costs for the next two years.

(b) What is the most appropriate action for Chris Davis to take?

	✓
Seek the advice of an expert with knowledge of the purchase and installation of car charging ports to assist with relevant costings.	✓
Complete the budget to the best of their abilities, but flex the budget in the second year to correct any issues.	
Ask Graham Musa, the purchasing manager, to build the budget, but add additional budgetary slack in place.	

(1 mark)

(c) Katrina Walter, the General Accounts Clerk and Cashier, has asked you to show whether the following would be detected by preparing a bank reconciliation.

A payment was made to Electro Vehicles Ltd rather than Volt plc	Would not ▼
A cheque payment to Greenside & Co has not yet been banked by the supplier	Would ▼
A transposition error was made when recording a receipt in the cash book	Would ▼
A prompt payment discount was available but was not taken advantage of when paying Hitech Cars Ltd	Would not ▼
A direct debit was processed by the bank but was omitted from the cash book	Would ▼

Picklist:

Would be detected
Would not be detected

(5 marks)

You have recommended that, for each payroll run, a total of the number of personnel on the payroll should be automatically checked to ensure no unauthorised amendments have been made to AEM Ltd's payroll.

(d) Which type of control is this?

	✓
A programmed control over standing data	✓
A general IT control	
An authorisation check	✗

(1 mark)

Your duties at AEM Ltd include preparing the inventories section of the financial statements. Chris Davies, the financial controller, instructed you at 3pm to have the inventories section prepared by the end of the day for his review. You have not received all the inventory count returns from the car showrooms yet, and you have questions outstanding regarding some of the inventory being held at the Wembley warehouse.

(e) Answer the following questions.

Which of your fundamental ethical principles is threatened by this request?

Professional ▼
Competence & Due care

Picklist:

Confidentiality
Objectivity
Professional competence and due care

What action should you take?

request more time & Assistance ▼
from Chris

Picklist:

You must comply with Chris's instruction as well as you can
You must request more time and assistance from Chris to complete the task
You must resign

(4 marks)

(f) Identify the MOST useful report required by the following stakeholders.

Potential new investors to the company	FS as filed ▼
Board of Directors	Balanced SC ▼
HM Revenue & Customs	Corp tax ▼

Picklist:

Balanced Scorecard of the company
Corporation tax return for the period
Financial statements as filed with the Registrar of Companies
Statement of cash flows
Statement of financial position

(6 marks)

Task 2 (20 marks)

This task contains parts (a) and (b).

(a) Match the appropriate category of internal controls to each description

(5 marks)

Description	Category of internal control
The way in which staffing levels and job descriptions are set by management to support internal control	▼ Organisational
Controls to ensure that transactions have been processed accurately and completely	▼ Arithmetic
Monitoring and support of individual staff members	Supervisory ▼
Oversight and review of control activities to ensure they are being carried out correctly	Management ▼
Appropriate recruitment, selection and training of staff	Personnel ▼

Picklist:

~~Personnel~~
Supervisory
Arithmetic
~~Organisational~~
Management

You have been asked to review the controls in the sales system at AEM Ltd. You have collected the following information:

Showroom sales

- The sales team in each showroom are responsible for interacting with customers and making sales.
- The target sales price for each vehicle is set by the Sales & Marketing Director, Barbara Sinta and this is entered onto the sales system by the Accounts Receivable Clerk.
- Most customers will negotiate with the sales person to try to drive the price down. The showroom manager can verbally approve any discount up to 5% of the target sales price. Any discounts in excess of 5% must be approved by the Sales & Marketing Director by email.
- Each member of the sales team has a quarterly sales target (after any discounts) and will receive a bonus for reaching that target. A bonus is also paid for getting more than 50% of customers to purchase the three-year servicing plan. Sales team members are paid minimum wage before their bonus.
- Customers either pay for the vehicle outright or pay for the vehicle in instalments over an agreed time period which is known as a finance agreement. When a vehicle is purchased under a finance agreement, 10% of the target sales price must be paid as a deposit.

Recording showroom sales

- When a sale is made, the sales team member inputs the sale directly onto the sales system.
- The sales team member has to change the price on the system if the vehicle has been sold for less than target price.
- Sales made under a finance agreement must be identified to ensure that the Credit Controller has the correct information to set up the finance agreement.
- Any customer can set up a finance agreement as long as they agree to pay the 10% deposit.
- The showroom manager reviews total sales entered onto the system at the end of each week. Managers check the total sales value recorded, the number of sales recorded and the percentage of servicing plans sold. No other details are checked.

Payments

- Payments, or deposits for vehicles are made by cash, debit or credit card.
- When cash payments are made, the sales team member is responsible for taking the cash to the bank as soon as possible after the sale is made.

Online sales

- The website displays vehicles at their target price.
- Vehicles are added regularly to the website by the Warehouse Manager.
- Customers are able to purchase any vehicle directly from the website without any human interaction if they pay the target price and pay the full amount up front by credit card.
- AEM Ltd commits to delivering vehicles within 24 hours of the completion of the sale, as long as the customer lives on mainland UK.
- Customers who purchase a vehicle with a finance agreement need to register their interest on the website. A member of the sales team based in Wembley will email them a copy of the finance agreement. Once the 10% deposit is paid, the vehicle will be delivered to the customer.
- When a vehicle is sold, it needs to be manually removed from the website. This is done once a week.

- If a customer has paid for a vehicle that is no longer available, the customer is refunded within 14 days.
- Credit card companies have 72 hours from the point of sale to alert AEM Ltd if a payment cannot be completed.

(b) Complete your review as follows, using the provided answer spaces below:

- **Identify FIVE systemic weaknesses in the company's internal controls for processing sales**
- **Explain how each weakness that you have identified could create a problem for the company.**

Note. You are **not** required to make recommendations to change procedures.

	Weakness (1 mark)	Impact on AEM Ltd (2 marks per well-explained impact)
1	Cash - Sales Team Responsible	- Result in fraud - cash stolen -
2	Car on Websit even if Sold	- Reputation - Refunds 14 days
3	Delivery within 24hrs	- Car could be delivered without Payment (72hrs CC)
4	No Credit Checks	- Client could not afford car/High debt already
5	approval of discounts	verbally up to 5%. not recorded not record = loss

(15 marks)

Task 3 (20 marks)

This task contains parts (a) to (d).

(a) Identify whether the following statements in relation to performance indicators are TRUE or FALSE.

Description	True	False
The working capital cycle is the period between when cash leave the business for production of a product or service and the collection of cash from a customer.	✓	
Return on capital employed is an indicator of investment efficiency, as it looks at how well a business has invested the capital available to it.	✓	
The trade payables payment period measure how long the business takes to receive payment from customers.		✓
The operating profit margin shows the amount of operating profit generated for every £1 of sales revenue. It gives an indication of how well expenses have been controlled by the business.	✓	
Asset turnover compares the sales revenue of a business to current assets. It shows the revenue generated from use of current assets.		✓

(5 marks)

(b) Identify whether the following costs are deemed to be relevant costs for Argent Electric Motors Ltd to expand their current network of showrooms.

	Relevant cost/Not relevant cost
Purchase costs of new showroom sites	▼
Costs of researching new electric vehicles (research and development)	▼
Website costs	▼
Recruitment costs for showroom staff	▼

Picklist

Relevant cost
Not relevant cost

(4 marks)

Tariq Khan, the sales manager, has prepared the following budgetary control report for the showroom sales in January.

Additional information

- Due to poor weather, there were fewer customer visits and sales were lower than expected.
- The fixed costs are the salary of the showroom managers and £20,000 per year of the electricity and gas costs. Depreciation is also a fixed cost.
- All showroom staff, with the exception of the showroom managers are paid hourly.
- Due to high inflation, costs of power and materials are rising.

(c) Flex the budget using the information provided

	Budget	Flexed budget	Actual	Variance Fav/(Adv)
Average vehicle target price	£25,000			
Sales volume	250		219	
	£000	£000	£000	£000
Sales revenue	6,250		5,650	
Costs				
Vehicle purchase	3,200		2,960	
Showroom staff costs	1,000		960	
Showroom electricity & gas - variable	60		68	
Showroom electricity & gas - fixed	20		20	
Showroom depreciation	250		252	
Showroom manager costs	400		430	
Total costs	4,930		4,690	
Operating profit	1,320		960	

(8 marks)

(d) Comment on the results and suggest reasons for the variances

(3 marks)

Task 4 (20 marks)

Alison Clockwell, the finance director, is preparing a presentation for the board of directors. She has asked you to complete a comparative 'score card' of key financial ratios which she will use as part of her presentation.

Relevant data has been extracted from the last two years' accounts.

Extracts from accounts of Argent Electric Motors Ltd	Year ended 31 December 20X2 £000	Year ended 31 December 20X1 £000
Sales revenue	40,230	36,580
Cost of sales	28,750	26,850
Profit from operations	2,380	3,430
Assets		
Non-current assets	2,170	1,730
Inventories	4,885	4,260
Trade receivables	950	640
Cash and equivalents	945	1,340
Total assets	**8,950**	**7,970**

Extracts from accounts of Argent Electric Motors Ltd	Year ended 31 December 20X2 £000	Year ended 31 December 20X1 £000
Equity and Liabilities		
Total equity	2,435	2,160
Non-current liabilities	3,200	2,400
Trade payables	2,955	3,075
Tax liabilities	360	335
Total equity and liabilities	**8,950**	**7,970**

(a) Complete the scorecard by calculating the missing ratios for the year ended 31 December 20X2.

Argent Electric Motors Ltd Scorecard	Year ended 31 Dec 20X2	Year ended 31 Dec 20X1	Industry average 20X2
Profitability and gearing (correct to 1 dp):			
Gross profit %	%	26.6%	28.0%
Operating profit %	5.9%	9.4%	10.6%
Return on capital employed	42.2%	75.2%	38.5%
Gearing	%	52.6%	60.0%
Liquidity ratios (correct to 1 dp):			
Current ratio	: 1	1.8 : 1	1.6: 1
Acid test/quick ratio	0.6 : 1	0.6 : 1	0.5 : 1
Working capital days (correct to nearest day):			
Inventory holding period	days	58 days	83 days
Trade receivables collection period	9 days	6 days	14 days
Trade payables payment period	38 days	42 days	45 days
Working capital cycle	days	22 days	52 days

(10 marks)

(b) Select the ONE most appropriate observation about each aspect of business performance below.

Profitability

	✓
The operating profit ratios decreased due to the additional fixed costs of the new head office.	
Operating profit ratios have decreased due to the increase in the cost of fruit and vegetables purchased by the company.	
Profitability has declined due to reduced sales and poor staff morale.	

(2 marks)

Return on capital employed

	✓
A new showroom was opened towards the end of 20X1 and the results of that have impacted ROCE in 20X2.	
Asset turnover has decreased in 20X2 due to the increase in borrowing.	
ROCE is better than the industry average due to better than average profitability.	

(2 marks)

Liquidity

	✓
Both ratios have increased which indicates that the company is less solvent.	
Both ratios remain too high, indicating that working capital is not being used effectively.	
The increase in inventory levels has had the most impact on the liquidity ratios.	

(2 marks)

Working capital

	✓
The payable days have reduced over the period, meaning it takes more time to pay suppliers.	
The cost of vehicles has increased by 10% in 20X2 although the number of vehicles in inventory is roughly constant leading to an increase in the inventory holding period.	
Working capital management is good compared to the inventory average and has improved since 20X1.	

(2 marks)

Overall performance

	✓
Profitability has declined in 20X2, due to increasing fixed costs. However, the liquidity measures show an improving financial position.	
Performance against industry averages is generally favourable apart from working capital management.	
20X2 has been a mixed year but the increase in debt has impacted the operating profit and liquidity.	

(2 marks)

Task 5 (20 marks)

This task contains parts (a) to (d).

(a) Match the appropriate cost type to each scenario when making short-term decisions

Scenario	Cost type
The cost of machinery purchased six months ago when comparing two projects that will both use the machine.	▼
Cost of lost customer revenue when considering organisational change	▼
The cost of new equipment when preparing a cost-benefit analysis	▼
The lost contribution from machinery that might have been purchased if the business had not invested in another project.	▼
The fixed supervisor cost that would be avoided if a product was no longer produced when product costing.	▼

Picklist:

Opportunity cost
Relevant cost
Intangible cost
Tangible cost
Sunk cost

(5 marks)

Management often consider a regular review of the current control system in place.

Argent Electric Motors Ltd has expanded its head office in Wembley, which has resulted in additional recruitment and additional costs.

(b) Explain why this situation may be a reason for management to review the controls at head office by commenting on the following key areas:

- **increased number of staff**
- **adequacy of the existing system**
- **the importance of monitoring controls**

Increased number of staff

(2 marks)

Adequacy of the existing system

(2 marks)

Monitoring of controls

(2 marks)

The following additional information has been provided.

Note. This part of the scenario will change in the live assessment, and is provided purely for practice.

Argent Electric Motors Ltd have employed the services of a consultant who has investigated the expected costs of a new procurement system. The following report has been prepared.

Dear Directors,

In response to your recent enquiry regarding changing your procurement system, I attach the following information for you.

I recommend that you change your current system and purchase a new system called Procure4Less. This package will allow orders to be placed directly with your preferred suppliers as it will interface directly with their systems. This is likely to result in a reduction in staffing levels in your finance team.

The recommended software, Procure4Less, can be purchased for £240,000. You will need to purchase some additional modules to ensure compatibility with your cloud accounting software at an additional cost of £14,000. Annual licence fees for Procure4Less are £4,500 and it is assumed that the software will be used for ten years as long as it is maintained and regularly updated.

The accounts payable module in your cloud accounting system, which cost £12,000, is fully compatible with Procure4Less once the modifications suggested have been made.

The change in procurement system will need to be managed with your suppliers. I recommend that your Accounts Payable team contact each supplier to ascertain if they have the correct software to interface with Procure4Less.

I estimate that it will take 20 working days for staff to make these checks at a daily staff cost of £260.

I recommend that you employ a software engineer on a short-term contract to manage the modification and installation of the software as well as providing staff training. This should take three months and the monthly cost of a software engineer would be £6,000.

The internal IT department will receive training and should be able to deal with any day-to-day queries with the software; however, the software engineer should perform an annual review and upgrade of the software which would cost £2,200.

Based on current levels, I estimate that you will be able to reduce the headcount in your payables team by 2 members of staff. I understand that the average salary of junior finance staff is £18,000 although redundancy costs of £4,000 per staff member are expected.

I enclose my invoice for the agreed fee of £1,200 for this report for your kind attention.

Do not hesitate to contact me if you have any further questions.

Yours sincerely,

Bella Dickson (IT consultant)

(c) Prepare a cost benefit analysis based on the information in the scenario and the additional information provided.

	£	£
Initial costs		
Annual running costs		
Savings/additional revenue		
Total net benefit/(cost) over 10 years		

(5 marks)

(d) Other factors to consider (non-financial) and a conclusion based on the assessment of the cost/benefit analysis.

(4 marks)

BPP PRACTICE ASSESSMENT 3
LEVEL 4 SYNOPTIC ASSESSMENT

ANSWERS

Level 4 Synoptic Assessment
BPP practice assessment 3: answers

Task 1 (20 marks)

(a) AEM Ltd has a centralised accounting function. The accounting function will produce management information such as budgets to help the directors with planning, decision making, controlling and performance measurement.

(3 marks)

(b)

	✓
Seek the advice of an expert with knowledge of the purchase and installation of car charging ports to assist with relevant costings.	✓
Complete the budget to the best of their abilities, but flex the budget in the second year to correct any issues.	
Ask Graham Musa, the purchasing manager, to build the budget, but add additional budgetary slack in place.	

The finance department has experience in the car retail industry, but adding on a new and specialised area such as the supply and installation of electric car charging ports will require additional help and assistance from an expert, such as a consultant.

Correcting the budget in the second year is to be expected, but again, the issue of not having the required knowledge to build a meaningful budget from the start will be the problem.

Asking the purchasing manager to build the budget without having the required knowledge of the expected costs and problems, the budget will not be built correctly. Completing the budget but adding in budgetary slack will potentially lead to poor cost control (as targets are too generous) or unmotivated staff (if targets are unobtainable).

(1 mark)

(c)

A payment was made to Electro Vehicles Ltd rather than Volt plc	Would not be detected
A cheque payment to Greenside & Co has not yet been banked by the supplier	Would be detected
A transposition error was made when recording a receipt in the cash book	Would be detected
A prompt payment discount was available but was not taken advantage of when paying Hitech Cars Ltd	Would not be detected
A direct debit was processed by the bank but was omitted from the cash book	Would be detected

Reconciliations are checks where staff ensure that two different sources of information agree, and that any differences are understood. So for a bank reconciliation, the differences between the bank statement and the cash book are investigated.

Therefore, payments made to the wrong customer would not be detected as the payments would tally on both sources.

Missing a prompt payment discount would not be identified as, again, both the cash book and the bank statement would agree.

The other errors would be detected as there would be a difference on the bank statement and the cash book.

(5 marks)

(d)

	✓
A programmed control over standing data	✓
A general IT control	
An authorisation check	

This will be a specific programme designed for the payroll data only to be verified – this may be in the form of an activity log report to show the details behind any amendments, or a specific alert when changes are made. This is an example of an application control.

General IT controls would cover the overall IT system security such as use of passwords or access permissions.

An authorisation check would occur between a user making the change and the change being activated on the system (alternatively, if using paper authorisation, there may be authorisation prior to entering the data).

(1 mark)

(e) Professional competence and due care

You must request more time and assistance from Chris to complete the task

(4 marks)

It is evident that you need more time to ensure that you have all the relevant information for preparing the inventories section of the financial statements to the best of your abilities. Without all the financial information, you cannot be expected to complete the work in the time given. You will need to advise Chris of the situation, maybe asking them to contact the Wembley warehouse for the missing information. Professional competence and due care requires the account to have not only sufficient skill, but sufficient time and resources to undertake the tasks.

(f)

Potential new investors to the company	Financial statements as filed with the Registrar of Companies
Board of Directors	Balanced Scorecard of the company
HM Revenue & Customs	Corporation tax return for the period

Potential new investors would only have access to information available in the public domain, this would mainly be financial statements filed at Companies House. Share prospectus information may also be available for new listings, but this isn't an option here.

HMRC are concerned with the tax information available from the company, so although they would also require a copy of the financial statements, it would be most useful for them to use the Corporation Tax information which specifically shows any deductions or allowances as well.

The Board of Directors would require different information regarding the performance of the company, available to those within the company. The balanced scorecard would enable them to see what areas are performing well, and the Board could request further information, such as cash flows; however, this is likely to be covered already, in more detail, in the scorecard report.

(6 marks)

Task 2 (20 marks)

(a) Match the appropriate category of internal controls to each description

Description	Category of internal control
The way in which staffing levels and job descriptions are set by management to support internal control	Organisational
Controls to ensure that transactions have been processed accurately and completely	Arithmetic
Monitoring and support of individual staff members	Supervisory
Oversight and review of control activities to ensure they are being carried out correctly	Management
Appropriate recruitment, selection and training of staff	Personnel

(5 marks)

(b)

	Weakness (1 mark)	Impact on AEM Ltd (2 marks per well-explained impact)
1	There is no formal recording of the approval of discounts.	If large discounts are given without authorisation, this will reduce revenue for the company and profit margins. Sales could become loss making.
2	The sales team bonus structure may incentivise fraud	Sales team members may be reliant on their bonus payments, and may manipulate the financial records to ensure they meet their targets. There is a risk that the financial records are falsified. Staff may also leave if they are do not feel supported and valued by the company, which would impact the balanced scorecard.

	Weakness (1 mark)	Impact on AEM Ltd (2 marks per well-explained impact)
3	There is no detailed review of sales entered onto the sales system.	The wrong sale amount could be entered after discount which would lead to revenue being recorded incorrectly. Customer details may be recorded incorrectly which might mean that customers on finance agreements do not make their finance payments.
4	There is no credit check for customers with finance agreements	There is a risk that customers may not be able to afford the repayments. AEM Ltd could lose a substantial amount of money if many customers default.
5	The sales team member is responsible for banking cash sales.	The sales team member could steal some or all of the cash. The cash could be lost or stolen if not stored securely.
6	Online vehicle listing is not up to date	Customers could purchase a vehicle that has already been sold. This could lead to reputational damage and significant levels of refunds.
7	Vehicles could be delivered and the card payment may not be completed.	Cars could be delivered without payment being made and AEM Ltd would not necessarily be able to reclaim that money.

Note. Only FIVE weaknesses were required.

(15 marks)

Task 3 (20 marks)

(a) Identify whether the following statements in relation to performance indicators are TRUE or FALSE.

Description	True	False
The working capital cycle is the period between when cash leave the business for production of a product or service and the collection of cash from a customer.	X	
Return on capital employed is an indicator of investment efficiency, as it looks at how well a business has invested the capital available to it.	X	
The trade payables payment period measure how long the business takes to receive payment from customers.		X
The operating profit margin shows the amount of operating profit generated for every £1 of sales revenue. It gives an indication of how well expenses have been controlled by the business.	X	
Asset turnover compares the sales revenue of a business to current assets. It shows the revenue generated from use of current assets.		X

(5 marks)

(b)

	Relevant cost/Not relevant cost
Purchase costs of new showroom sites	Relevant cost
Costs of researching new electric vehicles (research and development)	Not relevant cost
Website costs	Not relevant cost
Recruitment costs for showroom staff	Relevant cost

Relevant costs are the costs which are only incurred if the project goes ahead. Purchase cost of the new showrooms and the recruitment costs of the new showroom staff will only occur if a new showroom is opened. The website costs are sunk costs (these have already occurred) and the researching costs will occur regardless of whether the new showrooms are opened as this is needed for the existing business.

(4 marks)

(c)

	Budget	Flexed budget	Actual	Variance Fav/(Adv)
Average vehicle target price	£25,000			
Sales volume	250		219	
	£000	**£000**	**£000**	**£000**
Sales revenue	6,250	5,475	5,650	175
Costs				
Vehicle purchase	3,200	2,803	2,960	(157)
Showroom staff costs	1,000	876	960	(84)
Showroom electricity & gas - variable	60	53	68	(15)
Showroom electricity & gas - fixed	20	20	20	-
Showroom depreciation	250	250	252	(2)
Showroom manager costs	400	400	430	(30)
Total costs	4,930	4,402	4,690	(288)
Operating profit	1,320	1,073	960	(113)

(8 marks)

(d) Revenue

Revenue has fallen as the sales volume is lower than budgeted. However, there is a favourable revenue variance which indicates the average vehicle target sales prices was higher than the £25,000 budgeted.

Costs

There are adverse variances on all costs. The high level of inflation has resulted in higher vehicle purchase and variable electricity and gas costs. The vehicle purchase costs are the largest cost, and so any increase in prices will have a significant overall impact on the profit.

(3 marks)

Task 4 (20 marks)

(a)

Argent Electric Motors Ltd Scorecard	Year ended 31 Dec 20X2	Year ended 31 Dec 20X1	Industry average 20X2
Profitability and gearing (correct to 1 dp):			
Gross profit %	**28.5%**	26.6%	28.0%
Operating profit %	5.9%	9.4%	10.6%
Return on capital employed	42.2%	75.2%	38.5%
Gearing	**56.8%**	52.6%	60.0%
Liquidity ratios (correct to 1 dp):			
Current ratio	**2.0** : 1	1.8 : 1	1.6: 1
Acid test/quick ratio	0.6 : 1	0.6 : 1	0.5 : 1
Working capital days (correct to nearest day):			
Inventory holding period	**62** days	58 days	83 days
Trade receivables collection period	9 days	6 days	14 days
Trade payables payment period	38 days	42 days	45 days
Working capital cycle	**33 days**	22 days	52 days

(10 marks)

Workings

	Year ended 31 December 20X2 £000
Gross profit Gross profit/revenue ×100%	(40,230 – 28,750) / 40,230 × 100% = 28.5%
Gearing Non-current liabilities / (Non-current liabilities _+ equity)	3,200 / (3,200 + 2,435) = 56.8%
Current ratio Current assets / current liabilities : 1	(8,950 – 2,170) / (2,955 +360) : 1 = 2.0 : 1
Inventory holding period Inventory/cost of sales × 365	4,855 / 28,750 × 365 = 62 days
Working capital days Inventory holding days + trade receivables	

	Year ended 31 December 20X2 £000
collection period – trade payables payment period	62 days + 9 days – 38 days = 33 days

For a reminder on ratios, visit your *Financial Statements for Limited Companies* course book (Chapter 11).

(b) Profitability

	✓
The operating profit ratios have decreased due to the additional fixed costs of the head office.	✓
Operating profit ratios have decreased due to the increase in the cost of vehicles purchased by the company.	
Profitability has declined due to reduced sales and poor staff morale.	

Gross profit has increased over the period, so it is unlikely to be the cost of vehicles (which would be a cost of sales). Revenue has increased in the period, so it is not a reduction in sales. Operating costs would include the additional fixed cost of the new head office, and this is likely to have adversely affected the operating profit ratios.

(2 marks)

Return on capital employed

	✓
A new showroom was opened towards the end of 20X1 and the results of that have impacted ROCE in 20X2.	
Asset turnover has decreased in 20X2 due to the increase in borrowing.	✓
ROCE is better than the industry average due to better than average profitability.	

Opening a new showroom in 20X1 would increase the capital employed, but the returns would not be seen until 20X2. This would have the impact of increasing ROCE, but it has actually decreased.

Although gross profit margin is slightly higher than industry average in 20X2, ROCE is calculated on operating profit margin which is lower than the industry average. Therefore ROCE is better than industry average due to lower capital employed, rather than higher profitability.

Asset turnover (revenue / capital employed) has decreased in 20X2. Revenue has increased, but there has been an increase in borrowing which would increase capital employed.

(2 marks)

Liquidity

	✓
Both ratios have increased which indicates that the company is less solvent.	
Both ratios remain too high, indicating that working capital is not being used effectively.	
The increase in inventory levels has had the most impact on the liquidity ratios.	✓

One ratio has increased and one has remained steady which would suggest that the company is more, rather than less, solvent.

The current ratio has increased to 2.0 : 1 and the quick ratio has remained steady at 0.6 : 1. Neither of these ratios are particularly high and are only slightly higher than the industry average. They do not indicate ineffective use of working capital.

(2 marks)

Working capital

	✓
The payable days have reduced over the period, meaning it takes more time to pay suppliers.	
The cost of vehicles has increased by 10% in 20X2 although the number of vehicles in inventory is roughly constant leading to an increase in the inventory holding period.	✓
Working capital management is good compared to the inventory average and has improved since 20X1.	

Payables days have reduced, but that means it is taking less time to pay suppliers.

Working capital management is good compared with the inventory average but working capital days have increased by 50% compared to 20X1 indicating a decrease in working capital management.

An increase in inventory cost with a similar level of inventory could result in an increased inventory holding period.

(2 marks)

Overall performance

	✓
Profitability has declined in 20X2, due to increasing fixed costs. However, the liquidity measures show an improving financial position.	✓
Performance against industry averages is generally favourable apart from working capital management.	
20X2 has been a mixed year but the increase in debt has impacted the operating profit and liquidity.	

The working capital ratios are better than the industry averages, despite increases in inventory holding and receivables days. Performance against industry averages is favourable apart from operating profit margin.

The increase in debt would impact finance costs, but not operating profit margin as finance costs are deducted after operating profit.

The gross profit margin increased slightly but operating profit margin decreased, indicating that fixed costs are likely to have increased. The liquidity measures have improved slightly.

(2 marks)

Task 5 (20 marks)

(a) Match the appropriate cost type to each scenario when making short-term decisions

Scenario	Cost type
The cost of machinery purchased six months ago when comparing two projects that will both use the machine.	Sunk cost
Cost of lost customer revenue when considering organisational change	Intangible cost
The cost of new equipment when preparing a cost-benefit analysis	Tangible cost
The lost contribution from machinery that might have been purchased if the business had not invested in another project.	Opportunity cost
The fixed supervisor cost that would be avoided if a product was no longer produced when product costing.	Relevant cost

(5 marks)

(b) Increased number of staff

If existing staff have been promoted to manage the new recruits they may need training in ensuring that they understand what is meant by controls and how they need to monitor these controls.

It is important that new staff are given sufficient training or support to do their jobs effectively including necessary control procedures.

Adequacy of the existing system

Controls that exist in the current system may no longer be fit for purpose. As Argent Electric Motors Ltd has grown, there may be deficiencies in the system. For example, the payroll will have grown significantly, so are the current staff coping with the changes? It is essential that the suppliers are paid on time, not only to ensure an effective flow of vehicles but also to make sure that the company is maintaining its high ethical standards.

A company which has undergone a significant amount of change will need to assess their controls on a regular basis to keep up with the changes within the business and to minimise errors or loss.

Monitoring of controls

The monitoring of controls is essential otherwise there is a risk that the controls will not be adhered to by staff. Without monitoring of controls, there is an additional risk of fraud going undetected or errors being missed.

(6 marks)

(c) Cost benefit analysis

	£	£
Initial costs		
Purchase of software	(240,000)	
Purchase of additional modules	(14,000)	
Supplier checks (20 × £260)	(5,200)	
Software engineer installation/training (3 × £6,000)	(18,000	
		(277,200)
Annual running costs		
Licence fee (10 × £4,500)	(45,000)	
Annual upgrade (10 × £2,200)	(22,000)	
Total costs over 10 years		(67,000)
Savings/additional revenue		
Staff savings (2 staff × 10 years × £18,000) – (2 × £4,000 redundancy costs)	352,000	
		352,000
Total net benefit/(cost) over 10 years		7,800

(5 marks)

(d) Other factors to consider (non-financial) and a conclusion based on the assessment of the cost/benefit analysis.

The change in procurement system shows that there is a small overall net benefit of making the change. However, small changes to the proposed costs may reduce that benefit.

If the current supplier is unable to interface with the new system then its benefit is reduced. Key suppliers should be contacted prior to any purchase to ensure that their systems are compatible.

Some savings could be made on the costs of the software engineer if there are any inhouse staff who were able to take on this role; however, that will have an impact on their current workload.

There is no cost currently included for staff training as staff will be unable to perform their role while undertaking training.

The success of the system is based on the compatibility with supplier systems so it is vital that this work is carried out before a final decision is made. However, based on the evidence provided it would appear to be a good investment to install the new system.

(4 marks)

Note. The conclusion can be positive or negative in its recommendation, provided that the answer is justified and considers both the financial and the non-financial criteria required in a cost benefit analysis. Three marks are awarded for suggesting suitable non-financial factors and one mark for a supported conclusion.

Tell us what you think

Got comments or feedback on this book? Let us know.
Use your QR code reader:

Or, visit:
https://www.smartsurvey.co.uk/s/GPUBYI/

Need to get in touch with customer service?

www.bpp.com/request-support

Spotted an error?

https://learningmedia.bpp.com/pages/errata